> You gain strength, courage and confidence
> by every experience in which you really stop to look fear in the face.
> You must do the thing you think you cannot do.

Anna Eleanor Roosevelt
11 Oct 1884 – 7 Nov 1962

Sofa to Singapore
Conquering Solo Travel Anxiety

Gordon Chesterman

www.pinkbeebooks.com

About Me

▶ I am by no means a psychiatrist, psychologist, therapist or any type of 'ist'. I just know what worked for me. We wouldn't be interacting right now if it wasn't for travelling to Singapore. I hadn't thought about writing this book at all. The idea simply popped in to my head in my hotel room while transferring the photos I had taken that day to my laptop. I thought, maybe my experiences can help someone else to overcome their fears of travelling alone.

I once again felt amazed and thrilled to be back in Singapore, wandering around taking photos—which I love doing. I was proud of myself for the months of researching, planning, budgeting, looking for flights, hotels, and everything else in between.

You should know that by nature, I am very much a creature of habit. I like routine, so I become easily unnerved by sudden changes to what I'm expecting. I'm not full OCD, I just don't like surprises. I prefer being in general control and planning as much as I can because it feels comforting and reassuring.

Let's move forward to break those sofa shackles!

There are people who easily accept change, love surprises, and make friends at the drop of a hat. Well, I'm not that type of person. I'm shy, hardly ever comfortable in social situations and generally very wary of people and their intentions. As a result, I can understand your challenges as a shy or introverted person. However, I'm now quite used to travelling alone and exploring on my own terms.

With all that said, the aim of my book is to help you build the foundations of personal confidence, which may not feel natural, but it's hidden away deep down inside you somewhere. The trick is taking gentle baby steps, practising, and breathing deeply!

Keep in mind there is no magic formula for each and every personal situation because we are all different. However, I hope this book may help to change your life for the better so the thought of travelling on your own doesn't make you break out in a cold sweat anymore. Change can sometimes be difficult, but it can happen once you put your mind to it.

INTRODUCTION

If you are reading this book, you are probably yearning to go on holiday. However, for whatever reason or circumstance, you may find yourself on your own, without a travel buddy or partner to accompany you on your adventure. In addition, you may be an introvert or naturally shy and feeling anxious about exploring the world on your own.

Right now, you may feel awkward by your situation or that you are the only one experiencing travel fears. In reality, many people struggle with the same fears, anxieties, and insecurities, especially when considering solo travel. The idea of being thrust into unfamiliar environments without a familiar face may feel overwhelming. It might leave you imagining endless worst-case scenarios—what if you feel lonely? What if something goes wrong and you have no one to lean on?

These concerns are all valid and shared by countless others who desire adventure yet find themselves shackled by these heavy mental chains.

But imagine for a moment what it would be like to break free from those chains. Imagine stepping off the plane onto new soil, taking in foreign landscapes and cultures. As daunting as it may seem, embracing solo travel holds an amazing potential for transformation. You can discover strengths you never knew you had, cultivate resilience by overcoming challenges, and gain confidence from navigating the world independently. More than just getting from point A to point B, each journey will be a discovery about who you are and what you are capable of. When you return home, you'll have stories and experiences that inspire yourself and others.

That's exactly what you'll learn and why I have written this book. It's specifically designed for introverts, the socially anxious, and anyone who's ever felt sidelined by their fears of facing the world alone. It isn't about turning you into someone else or expecting you to shed your natural inclinations and anxieties completely. It's about finding empowerment and navigating through them with newfound wisdom, belief and strategies. Each chapter will address various aspects of solo travel anxiety while nurturing your confidence to transform what once seemed frightening, into something exciting.

I'll discuss how to deal with anxieties and negative feelings, build safety nets, and form itineraries which maintain and expand your comfort zone. I'll explain strategies to handle unexpected situations and solve problems you may not have foreseen. You can view this book as a step-building guide to developing social skills and self-confidence, ultimately fostering personal growth and self-discovery. That's quite a mouthful, but don't worry—the information will build up slowly without causing mass brain indigestion. ■

First, I'll address some of the main worries which may be on your mind—how to handle the logistics of travel planning without becoming overwhelmed, how to ensure personal safety, and how to embrace solitude rather than fear loneliness. Then, we will explore practical tools and insights tailored to help you manage social interactions. Whether it's striking up a conversation with locals, befriending fellow travellers, or simply enjoying solo moments of peace, you will learn how to navigate each situation with consummate ease. We will also explore ways to create meaningful experiences on your terms so you don't just see places—you truly experience them.

Finally, We will cover tips on maintaining your adventurous spirit once you are back home. The goal is to keep nurturing your newfound confidence and apply it to different aspects of your life, ensuring that the escape from your comfort zone extends beyond mere solo travel—a continuous journey of self-discovery and enrichment. ■

Relax & Enjoy

© Gordon Chesterman

CONTENTS

Understanding solo travel anxieties — 11
The fears we all have........................... 11
Facing common psychological barriers.......... 13
Challenging your fears before leaving........... 13
Fear journalling................................ 13
Ask for feedback............................... 13
Join communities (online and offline)........... 14
Learn to interact with others.................... 14
Dining alone.................................... 15
Visualisation techniques........................ 15
Building self-reliance and independence........ 15

Building up your confidence — 19
Find joy in solo activities....................... 19
Trust your decisions............................ 21
Coping with unexpected travel challenges...... 22
Mindfulness and gratitude to
enhance your experience...................... 23
Gratitude journalling........................... 23
Self-reflection................................. 24
Tuning into your senses........................ 24

Embracing solitude, not loneliness — 27
Loneliness vs. solitude......................... 27
Using loneliness to understand yourself........ 28
Balance connections with independence....... 30

Mentally preparing for your journey — 33
Opening up gradually.......................... 33
Set personal goals............................. 34
Visualise success.............................. 35

Crafting your perfect itinerary — 37
Select the right destination.................... 37
Talking about safety........................... 38
Practical preparations before departure........ 39
Gather information from different sources..... 42
Incorporate downtime for rest and reflection... 43
Balancing structure and spontaneity........... 44

Mastering travel logistics — 51
Choose the right accommodation.............. 51
Handle airport procedures with confidence.... 53
Use public transport safely and efficiently..... 55
Manage accommodation bookings
when plans change............................ 57

Health and wellness abroad — 61
Sustain healthy habits......................... 61
Strategise access to healthcare services...... 62
Prepare for potential emergencies............ 63
How to deal with common travel health issues... 64

Effective money management — 67
Form a realistic budget........................ 67
Adopt smart saving techniques................ 68
Safeguard finances against scams and theft... 70

Aleximx - AdobeStock

Ensuring safety on the road — 75
- Stay aware and adjusted to your surroundings — 75
- Protect personal belongings — 77
- Connect regularly with friends and family — 78
- Understand local customs — 79

Tips for female travellers — 82
- Pack specialised travel equipment — 84
- Tailored safety strategies — 84
- Build connections and support networks — 85
- Choose women-friendly tour operators and accommodations — 86

Cultivating hobbies to enhance your experience — 91
- A beginner's guide to travel photography — 91
- Practical tips for newbies — 92
- Ideas for journal-keeping — 94
- Hiking for independence — 95
- Immersive language learning — 96

Connecting via group activities — 101
- Guidelines for selecting group tours — 101
- Cooking and culinary experiences — 102
- Exploring artistic talents — 103
- Practising live sketching — 105
- Volunteering — 106

Tips for meaningful social interactions — 109
- Building authentic relationships on the road — 109
- Tips for balancing socialising and solitude — 110
- How to befriend locals and fellow travellers — 111
- Integrating with local communities — 114

Returning home and reflecting on your journey — 117
- Bringing travel experiences into your daily life — 117
- Enhancing relationships post-travel — 119
- Applying travel-gained skills — 119
- Sharing travel experiences to inspire others — 120

Long-term benefits of solo travel — 125
- Continue growing through new travels — 125
- Becoming more flexible — 126
- Building a toolkit of resources — 128
- Continuous learning and self-improvement — 128

Conclusion - Taking everything onboard — 131

References — 134

MeepianGraphic - Adobestock

"The Fears We All Have"

CHAPTER 1

Understanding solo travel anxieties

We all need a little dose of courage when stepping out of our comfort zone, but this is especially true for those of us who are naturally introverted, shy, or anxious. Instead of focusing on all the amazing things we could learn by exploring and imagining how our lives could change for the better, we may get stuck on the negatives. From the silliest thoughts, like jumping on the wrong plane, to the most frightening situations, such as getting lost in an unknown city, we may experience a variety of negative feelings and sensations.

In this chapter, we'll dive into the heart of these anxieties and take a close look at where they come from. We'll explore different types of fears which every introverted solo traveller battles and get down to understanding them from different angles. We'll also learn how these worries play out in our minds and impact our travel decisions. Then, we'll unpack some practical tips to manage these concerns.

The fears we all have

You might have already thought about the first solo travel you'll undertake. Maybe you've already imagined the destination, what you want to see there, and the things you want to try. Everything looks perfect in your mind, but you still struggle to make that first real step and book a flight. Your fears stop you from taking concrete actions and achieving your goals. We've all been there, procrastinating the departure indefinitely. But if you don't want to sit on your sofa for the rest of your life, it's time to manage your concerns. Let's begin by understanding which fears we're talking about.

The most common one is certainly the fear of getting lost. All travellers have it, but those with a companion probably struggle to understand its intensity. At least they know they can count on their friend or partner to support them in such

Ricky Kharawala - Unsplash

stressful moments. For those of us who travel alone, the situation is completely different. Would we be able to ask for directions if we don't speak the language? Do we have good enough orientation skills to understand where to go? These are just some of the questions that fill our minds. If you like to be in control as I do, you might be used to researching locations in advance, say on Google Earth, and considering every possible detail. So, if you've already thought about your first solo travel, you've probably found the perfect accommodation, watched many YouTube videos on what to do and see there, and read numerous articles. So, what else can you do? You'll discover this in the next sections.

Another common concern is safety, especially for women. In fact, a recent survey on solo female travel trends found that 70% of

Elnur - AdobeStock

respondents expressed concerns about safety *(2024 Solo Female Travel Trends & Statistics, 2024)*. Such worries might deter would-be adventurers from even booking a trip. However, understanding safety statistics and effective planning can significantly reduce these anxieties. For instance, research shows people who have travelled solo more than 10 times worry less about safety than those new to the experience. Sometimes, the most effective way of managing concerns is simply to keep doing something until you become more confident in your skills.

Loneliness is also a cause of anxiety for many solo travellers. Just picturing yourself on your own in a new country might make you feel nervous. This is completely understandable, as many people enjoy being close to their loved ones and know someone will always be there for them. My time of living and working abroad on my own made me used to being away from my family for long periods, but occasionally I've felt lonely too during my solo travels. Over the years, I've understood the difference between loneliness and solitude and embraced the latter. Moreover, I've realised how travelling alone offers plenty of opportunities to meet interesting people, connect with locals, and build self-confidence. If you've never embarked on a journey by yourself, you might struggle to understand how enriching this experience is. But you'll probably have an idea after reading this book.

Another fear we all have is the fear of social judgement. Unfortunately, society may tell us we should all have a partner or at least share our experiences with loved ones, so solo travel is usually perceived as a last resort rather than a deliberate choice. If you've talked about your desire to travel on your own, someone may have told you something such as, "Oh, you want to travel on your own? Don't you have anyone you can go with?" or "That must be amazing! I'm just sorry you have to travel by yourself and can't enjoy the experience with someone you love." These people may not understand that travelling alone is empowering and allows you to discover yourself deeply. In other words, being on your own isn't as bad as someone thinks. Many people are used to travelling alone—including me—and they have no problem with it. Instead, they find it incredibly satisfying and life-changing.

Facing common psychological barriers

In addition to common fears, there are some psychological barriers that we all need to face sooner or later if we want to get out of our comfort zone. They're sort of invisible chains which prevent us from exploring the world on our own. We may see them as insurmountable obstacles, but in reality, they just represent a negative self-perception or self-protection.

As an introverted and shy person, you may judge yourself harshly and question your skills and worth. You might even doubt yourself and believe you'll never be able to travel alone because you don't know how to get around on your own. Guess what? You can. Everybody can. That's because we're not a set of fixed skills, but we're capable of improving and achieving our goals. By putting yourself into it, you can learn to face challenges by yourself and build your self-confidence.

If you doubt yourself, you're also likely to fear the unknown. The unpredictability and uncertainty associated with new destinations

Take a leaf from Nature. Growing confidence slowly – is the key

and cultures may increase your anxiety and hinder your ability to grow and have unforgettable experiences. As you'll learn over the next chapters, balancing preparation and spontaneity is fundamental to overcoming the fear of the unknown. Being prepared certainly reduces some concerns, but opening yourself up to improvisation enriches your travel

experience and allows you to learn new things about yourself and the world around you. You may believe spontaneity can only worsen your anxiety, but it produces the opposite effect.

Last but not least is cognitive distortions can impact our self-perception and anxieties. These are negative thought patterns concerning our skills and qualities. There are different ones, like catastrophising or all-or-nothing thinking. Catastrophising involves imagining and focusing on only the worst-case scenarios, thus neglecting the positive events that may occur. For example, you may believe that if you take a flight to another part of the world on your own, your plane will surely crash, or you'll regret your choice the moment you land. All-or-nothing thinking, on the other hand, implies seeing everything in black or white. Therefore, you imagine your solo travel as being perfect or a catastrophe—you don't consider possible options in the middle.

Becoming aware of the mental barriers which can influence the perception of yourself is the first step to challenging them. Next, you can practise some simple yet useful exercises at home to build your confidence before actually going on holiday.

Challenging your fears before leaving

Some people might tell you, "Just go out there, and all your fears will disappear!" Although it's certainly true that having first-hand experiences improves your self-confidence, I wouldn't suggest starting this way. Your anxieties may worsen if and when you make mistakes and don't know how to face difficult situations on your own. So, let's start from the basics. If you really want to go on adventures alone, you should prepare from the comfort of your home and places where you live and gradually build up your skills.

Fear journalling

One effective method is fear journalling. This exercise involves writing down all your worries about travelling alone, no matter how big or small. The act of putting your thoughts on paper helps you clarify your feelings and identify recurring themes. When reading back, you'll likely notice patterns that reveal deeper insights into your anxiety. For example, if you're repeatedly worried about being lonely in a foreign country, this journal can serve as a reflection point for addressing that particular concern.

To get you started with fear journalling, set aside time each day to write without judgement or censorship. Let your thoughts flow freely, and focus on describing your fears and the scenarios that amplify them. Be brutally honest with yourself and don't bottle things up. Remember, this is not about finding immediate solutions but understanding your emotional triggers. Over time, this practise reduces the power these fears hold over you, making them easier to manage.

Ask for feedback

In addition to practising self-reflection, you can open yourself up and ask for others' feedback.

The easiest place to start is with your family and best friends. Share your fears and concerns with them and see how they react and what suggestions they make. Consider it a sort of "home therapy." They might not only offer reassurance but also encourage you to see things from different perspectives. At the same time, they can provide constructive feedback to help you prepare effectively for your solo travel.

If you don't know where to start, consider discussing your goal of travelling alone with someone you love and trust. Clarify what you want to do and express your concerns openly. Then, ask questions such as, "What would you do in my situation?" or "Have you ever found yourself in similar circumstances?" Don't be afraid to ask.

Join communities (online and offline)

Outside your circle of family and friends, there are many people who can help you address some or all your fears. Consider joining communities of like-minded fellow travellers, such as online forums, social media groups, or local meet-ups. Engaging with others who share similar fears normalises your anxiety, transforming it into an opportunity for connection and growth. If you don't feel comfortable talking in the beginning, it's absolutely fine. You can start by following conversations between others and intervene when you feel ready.

To prepare yourself, you can also join classes, which are another opportunity to meet people in the same boat. For example, if you want to go to Spain, think about joining a class to learn Spanish. It will naturally involve conversing with other people, thus breaking your barriers slowly but surely. I did exactly that before going to the Canary Islands by myself to live and work. I really enjoyed the classes and learned the usual basics, plus a reasonable standard off conversational phrases. When I arrived in Tenerife, I wasn't fluent by any means when talking to the locals, but they understood and loved the fact I was trying!

Learn to interact with others

If you doubt your abilities to handle conversations, you can follow some simple tips to achieve more self-confidence. First, learn more about body language. You can find many articles and YouTube videos which will teach you how to understand it. Being able to "read" people is an enormous help when you're on your own. It's also incredible fun! Just keep in mind that the interpretation of body language changes depending on the culture. So, make sure to focus on the country you want to go.

Body language also works in reverse, as I found out myself. One day, while visiting Singapore, I actually got lost believe it or not. I was so engrossed in taking photos that I hadn't made a mental note of where I was. So when I reached for my phone I realised I had left it in my hotel room on charge. Imagine seeing someone looking up at signs and turning around in circles with a vacant expression. Well, that was me in that moment. I appeared so lost that it didn't take long before someone noticed me. They obviously saw my dilemma and offered help before I had even decided to ask someone for directions.

In addition, practise some real-life experiments. You can try many different exercises to manage your concerns and change your self-perception. Take a trip into town around lunchtime and go into a cafe.

Don't choose an empty one, but one which is busy and quite full. This way, you force yourself to interact with others, such as asking if a seat is taken. Once seated, have a chat with the people nearby. You can simply say, "It's really busy in here, isn't it?" Then, two possible scenarios may occur: The other person just looks at you, nods, and keeps eating, or they start a conversation. In both situations, nothing bad happens but in the second one, you never know what positive outcomes you may achieve: You might get a friend for life or meet your future half—in which case, I've just made the rest of this book useless!

Another interesting experiment involves practising talking to staff when you go shopping. Use a "safety blanket" to feel more comfortable and not worry about how to act and what to say. A safety blanket is something that makes you feel at ease while interacting with others. In this particular case, it could be already knowing what you want to buy. Simply, go up to a staff member and ask them for help and advice. Then, look at their body language and how they react to your questions. This is not only fun but also builds your confidence to talk with complete strangers. Keep repeating this experiment in as many shops as possible until you really feel comfortable.

Dining alone

One of the most unsettling things is eating alone because it can be judged negatively by society. However, it's a scenario you'll probably have on holiday anyway, so why not try it in your hometown? Before practising this experiment, set small goals and divide them into steps.

Here's what you could try:

1 Have breakfast at a local café.

2 Have lunch in a busy café or pub.

3 Book dinner at a local restaurant.

4 Repeat the above steps until you feel totally comfortable.

5 Finally, treat yourself!
Book a table to dine alone at an exclusive restaurant or hotel near where you live.

As eating alone will probably be awkward the first few times, consider using your phone as a "digital safety blanket"— to pass the time. Next, try not to use the phone and practise people-watching. Then, if someone looks at you, try to keep eye contact and notice how they react in that split second. If they smile, smile back. If they don't react, keep watching elsewhere. Try not to attract the local psycho—that's where quickly assessing people comes into play and saves you!

Visualisation techniques

Alternatively, you can try some visualisation techniques which is mentally rehearsing positive travel experiences in your mind, which will eventually replace fear with confidence. Imagine yourself moving through a busy city with ease or relaxing at a beachside café. Create a vivid image focusing on the sights, sounds, and feelings associated with these moments. If you do it regularly, you rewire your brain to expect success, reducing anxiety when such situations arise in real life.

In order to practise this technique effectively, set a calm environment where you can focus undisturbed. Close your eyes and breathe deeply to clear your mind. Then, visualise a successful journey from start to finish, using all your senses. Picture overcoming obstacles effortlessly and savouring fulfilling interactions. Repeat this exercise daily, gradually building a reservoir of empowering mental images to draw upon when anxiety surfaces.

Building self-reliance and independence

Before setting out on your journey, you should know that your fears and concerns don't depend solely on your anxiety and personal challenges. Obviously, if you're

© Gordon Chesterman

naturally introverted, you struggle more than others to explore on your own. However, there are other factors that influence your negative thoughts. As already mentioned, family and community are prioritised over individual pursuits, solo travel is perceived as unusual or even undesirable. People tend to think they should stay as close as possible as fun and safe, while solo travel is risky and lonely. Therefore, it's normal to feel like doing something different when exploring on your own.

society plays a fundamental role in shaping our self-perceptions and decisions. If you become aware of the societal norms and expectations surrounding travel, you're more likely to overcome your fears and do what you want.

For instance, cultural norms can shape our ideas about who should and shouldn't travel alone. In many cultures, especially those where to their relatives and loved ones to support them and spend quality time together. Therefore, someone who decides to travel alone might be seen as "different" or "disrespectful" because they don't take care of their families.

Community perceptions and common stereotypes are strictly connected to cultural expectations. Society tends to depict group travel as you probably know, social media shapes our perceptions, too. We're often bombarded with amazing pictures from people we follow who travel and visit wonderful places, which sets expectations incredibly high. We imagine them having the best time of their lives with unforgettable experiences, forgetting the fact that everyone only shares the most memorable

moments. When we encounter the same situations in real life, we might expect everything to be perfect. If something goes wrong, we may feel inadequate, thus feeling more negative emotions. In reality, travel has its ups and downs, like everything else in life.

Finally, gender roles impact men and women differently. While men are expected to be adventurous and face dangerous situations on their own, women can be expected to stay safe and take care of their families and homes. This means that, on the one hand, men who feel anxious about travelling on their own may be seen as "weak," while women who decide to explore by themselves might be perceived as "uncaring" and "selfish."

Now, take a moment to reflect on the cultural norms that characterise your society: Do you think they're influencing your perception of solo travel? If so, acknowledge this. If the majority of people think that something is bad, it doesn't mean it is. I know it's hard to be different, but remember that there are many others around the world who face the same obstacles and decide to go on with their goals and aspirations. If you don't, you risk losing valuable opportunities to grow and become a better person.

To sum up, we have explored the most common fears and mental barriers associated with travelling alone. These concerns may seem daunting, but by acknowledging them, you can transform your travel experience into a rewarding journey. Understanding that these worries are shared by many can be comforting, and the strategies outlined offer practical methods to reduce any anxiety and boost confidence.

Remember, the exercises you learnt won't make your anxieties go away completely. Even though I have travelled alone a lot, I still have some issues. However, I've learnt to manage them to make sure I enjoy every moment. These and the next exercises are not about removing all your anxieties but effectively controlling them so that they don't interfere with your plans. During your travels, you'll have good and not so good experiences, but that's perfectly normal. The most important thing is that you learn to deal with your negative feelings in a positive way.

Fears are not for dwelling on, that's simply wasted emotional energy. They exist for us to understand and face them. They might appear destructive, but you are on the right path to making them constructive. You can be proud of yourself because it takes personal courage to become self-aware and face your fears. You might have never taken this action before, but you are now.

In the following chapter, we will go deeper into activities to help build up your self-confidence before going on holiday and learn to enjoy this life-changing experience. ■

CHAPTER 2

Building up your confidence

Building confidence begins with little steps, like taking a walk in the park alone—with safety in mind of course—or enjoying a quiet meal by yourself. These simple moments are the foundation of self-reliance and personal empowerment. They gently nudge you out of your comfort zone, encouraging you to trust your own instincts and savour your own company.

In this chapter, let's explore how these small, solitary experiences are not just acts of independence but pivotal exercises in decision-making. Through them, you'll gain insight into your preferences and learn to embrace your choices without second-guessing. You'll delve into various activities which promote spending quality time alone and discover how practising mindfulness boosts your confidence by grounding you in the present moment, thus reducing anxieties. You'll also learn techniques to make decisions independently and strategies to handle unexpected challenges on your travels.

The idea is to shift from feeling anxious about solitude to finding joy and assurance in it. By the end, you'll see how these skills not only

© Gordon Chesterman

make your solo adventures more enjoyable but also enrich your daily life, giving you the courage to explore the world on your terms.

Find joy In solo activities

Before going on a travel on your own, you should learn to enjoy spending time alone and appreciate your own company at home. Maybe you're already used to practising some activities by yourself, but you don't dedicate too much time to them. Exploring opportunities gives you insights into trying different things and adding more solo practises to your routine.

Solo hobbies such as painting, sculpting or writing are creative outlets which allows space for introspection. When you immerse yourself in creating art or crafting

cooking

what to do with my hands etc. Have you ever experienced something similar? In these cases, I enjoy having a camera hanging around my neck, sometimes even two or three. They are my safety blanket and a physical barrier between me and the rest of the world. If you explore solo activities, you may find something similar which makes you feel protected and motivates you to travel by yourself.

Everyday activities such as cooking can have impressive effects on your sense of independence. Obviously, cooking is an essential

stories, you aren't just expressing yourself; you're also learning to enjoy your own thoughts and ideas without justification. This way, you shift the focus from anxiety about being alone to a passion for what you love doing. It nurtures and encourages you to find out what truly piques your interest.

For example, my favourite hobby is photography. I love taking photos and shooting timelapses. Plus, it helps me step out of my comfort zone and explore the world. I have a deep-rooted anxiety about being stared at and feel awkward in front of strangers, usually not knowing

painting

photography

life skill we should all learn to be truly independent. But it's also much more than that; it's an act of self-care and empowerment. It's about making decisions based solely on your preferences, experimenting with new recipes, and relishing the satisfaction of a meal prepared in solitude. Even if you think you can't cook, just give it a try. In the beginning, we all make mistakes and may prepare not-so-delicious meals. But if you keep practising, you become better at it and learn to enjoy it - and the meal.

Another solo activity that can be extremely helpful before travelling alone is exploring local areas by yourself. Wander around town or visit nearby attractions—you may be surprised by what you discover! This way, you interact with new situations without the fear or anxieties associated with being far from home. You know you can go back to the comfort of your sofa, so you feel more relaxed and enjoy the experience. Exploring local areas by yourself is also a great way of understanding how you behave when you're alone in unfamiliar settings. It's the first step to becoming aware of who you are outside of your normal routine and what skills you have.

When walking in your hometown, you can try an experiment: Note if there are new shops which have recently opened. If so, just go in to experience something different. Technically, you're stepping out of your comfort zone. Even if the new shop, bar, or business in general doesn't interest you, just give it a try. It's also a good opportunity to have conversations with staff who may come up to you and ask if you need any help.

For example, I love museums and art galleries, because my mind is stimulated by shapes, colours, and light and shadows. One time, when I was wandering around my hometown, I noticed a guided tour with a small group of people. I followed them at a distance to gauge what the subject was. Gradually I walked closer to the group. Eventually, I made eye contact with the guide while she was talking. Finally, I moved closer, and the next thing I knew, the guide welcomed me by saying, "Please, join us" with a gentle wave of her hand. Suddenly, everyone was looking at me, I felt so awkward. But then, some of them shuffled apart to let me in with smiles so I started feeling more at ease. This unexpected circumstance allowed me to make polite conversation and even ask questions—which isn't usually like me. I truly enjoyed it!

In addition to exploring your hometown, attend events on your own, such as concerts, plays, or exhibitions, to show yourself you're capable of handling social settings. I know it can feel a bit scary, but it gives you the opportunity to truly enjoy an event. Think about all the times you arrived late because one of your friends had a last-minute issue or you didn't manage to really enjoy an activity because you were with someone else. If you participate in events on your own, you take your time and decide everything *you* want to do when *you* want to do it.

All these solitary activities strengthen the relationship you have with yourself and reinforce self-sufficiency. As you become used to engaging with the world independently, initial discomfort begins to fade, and you start feeling free. At the same time, you reflect on how you perceive yourself and understand that your worth and happiness don't always rely on constant companionship.

© Gordon Chesterman

Trust your decisions

You may feel overwhelmed when you have to make big decisions such as booking a flight or selecting the perfect accommodation. You have to consider so many factors and have so many doubts that you simply freeze and don't know what to do. This is what happens if you don't learn to make decisions on your own gradually. It's important to take one step at a time, starting with small daily decisions. If you think about it, you already handle a lot of them without even noticing. You decide what to eat for dinner, when to wake up, and what to do on the weekend. Pay attention to all the choices you make every day and become aware of your decision-making skills. Then, think about ways to test your abilities by

GOING ROUND IN CIRCLES TRYING TO SOLVE PROBLEMS - ARRGG!

In my case, the decision to go on holiday to Tenerife with a couple of friends opened an unexpected door a few years later. One of my friends had relatives there. I got along with them so well they said I could visit them anytime and that's exactly what I did. Eventually, their knowledge helped me get in touch with a local graphic design company, and I had to make an important decision: Stay in the UK or move to Tenerife to work. In the end, I decided to take a leap of faith and lived there for many years. You never know what amazing things might happen when you travel!

If you still struggle to make decisions and feel overwhelmed by them, start by completing simple tasks like pros and cons lists. I know this is a very simple technique, but have you really tried it? Writing down the pros and cons of a choice clears your mind and helps you evaluate situations objectively without trying to juggle it all in your head. This way, you have a rational basis which allows you to build your confidence and gradually trust your instincts. You can also try the visualisation techniques to feel less overwhelmed and anxious, as you learnt in Chapter 1.

Coping with unexpected travel challenges

As in life, travel always has its ups and downs. However, being prepared to face the "downs" helps you build the confidence to turn potential setbacks into mere bumps on the road.

The best action you can take is to create contingency plans to alleviate possible fears about the unknown. In other words, always prepare a plan B. For instance, consider alternatives if you miss a connection or the accommodation you chose is overbooked. Have a backup in mind, such as another place to stay or alternative routes you can take. Research suggests that travellers who book accommodation with 24-7 front desk services face fewer

increasing the difficulty of your decisions, such as planning a solo one-day trip somewhere close or scheduling activities you enjoy for one week or more.

To grow confidence gradually, consider past decisions that had positive outcomes. Reflect on moments when you had to make a choice and did it right. Perhaps you once decided to attend an event which opened doors to amazing opportunities or were at a crossroads in life and took the right turn choosing a new job or a new place to live. Don't underestimate your decisions; instead, learn to appreciate them and give credit to your decision-making skills when you deserve it. Even mistakes provide invaluable lessons, so think about past failures and how they changed your life for the better in one way or another.

safety concerns compared to those in remote lodgings *(8 Practical Tips to Overcome the Unexpected Hurdles of Solo Travel, 2024)*. This kind of proactive planning makes you feel in control over unpredictable events and provides peace of mind.

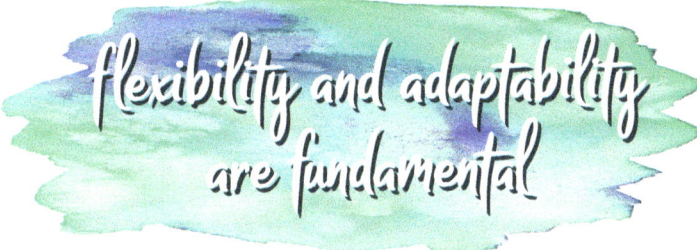

flexibility and adaptability are fundamental

In addition, you can role-play potential mishaps with friends before embarking on your journey. For example, imagine losing your luggage or having to interact with someone who doesn't speak your language. Think about possible scenarios you may encounter and prepare yourself with the help of someone you trust. If you practise distressing situations in a safe environment, you develop familiarity and problem-solving skills that might come in handy when you face the same scenarios in real life.

Another common strategy among solo travellers is to use travel apps. You can find everything online, from translators to apps that help navigation with useful information about local customs. If you want, you can combine this technique with the previous one, practising using a translation app with your friends.

However, no matter how much you prepare—you'll never be able to predict everything. For instance, you may resolve a language issue with your friend using apps, but when you try the same thing in real life, the locals struggle to understand you. Therefore, flexibility and adaptability are fundamental. When you're travelling on your own, embrace opportunities which arise unexpectedly or take advice from locals or experienced travellers to understand the best thing to do.

You must accept the fact that travel inherently comes with unpredictability. This way, you shift your mindset from dreading possible mishaps to viewing them as elements of the adventure. Adopting a flexible attitude allows you to embrace unforeseen circumstances instead of fearing them.

Mindfulness and gratitude to enhance your experience

But how can you become more flexible and accept unexpected events? The most effective way of doing this is by practising mindfulness. You've probably heard of this technique, and may even think of it as a bit cheesy, but it is very popular. Mindfulness is an ancient practise that allows you to stay present in the moment without overthinking the past or future. Thanks to it, you learn to reshape your thoughts and stop focusing on the destructive negative ones. You replace negativity with positivity and accept life as it is. As you might guess, it's especially helpful if you struggle with anxiety.

In fact, numerous scientific studies have linked present-moment awareness to a plethora of health benefits, including lower levels of perceived stress, anxiety, and depression *(Mindful Staff, n.d.)*. Being anchored in the present enhances your ability to respond to stressful situations effectively and translates into more reliance on your core values and greater perceived competence in handling various challenges. Through mindful living, you cultivate a sense of well-being which supports your confidence and resilience.

Mindfulness is characterised by numerous exercises which you can integrate into your daily life before leaving for your adventure. Here are some of them.

Gratitude journalling

Gratitude journalling is one effective method to explore solo hobbies and reduce your concerns about travelling alone. Reflect on moments that make you feel happy and write them down in your journal, such as spending quality time with yourself or making a small step toward preparing for your solo travel. Then, express gratitude for these good things in your life. You can note something like, "I'm grateful for my friend who, today, listened to my concerns about travelling alone" or "I'm grateful for the coffee I took this morning by myself in my favourite café." By practising gratitude, you gradually shift your mindset and learn to focus on the positives rather than the negatives. You can start by a stressful situation at work and told yourself to calm down and take a deep breath. It allows you to stay calm and focused on the here and now, thus assessing the situation objectively and making the best decision. There are many different breathing exercises that you can try. The structure is always the same:

1. Find a quiet place where you feel at ease and won't be disturbed.
2. If you feel comfortable, close your eyes.
3. Focus on your breathing, noticing how the air comes in and leaves your body.
4. Reflect on the real physical sensations you experience.
   - Is the air that comes in warmer than the air that leaves your body?
   - Is your breathing deep or shallow?
   - How does your body move as you inhale and exhale?
5. Continue to focus on your breathing for as much time as you want.

To make the activity easier, you can set a timer before starting. If you've never practised mindfulness before, start with two or three minutes and gradually dedicate more time to it.

After understanding the basic structure of breathing exercises, you can try various techniques. They include inhaling slowly, holding briefly, and exhaling; inhaling, holding, and exhaling.

In the beginning, you can try the above exercises when you feel calm and in a safe environment. As you get used to them, practise them in more stressful situations until they become second nature, so you naturally manage to relax by focusing on your breathing.

Self-reflection

Regularly reflecting on what happens in your life is another powerful strategy to shift your focus from negative thoughts to more positive ones. If you want, write down your ideas. Otherwise, simply dedicate a few minutes at the end of each day to recalling what happened. Consider what went well and how you handled various situations to highlight your personal, daily achievements and areas of improvement.

Avoid depicting failures and mistakes as bad; instead, view them as opportunities to do better the next day. Acknowledge that each experience you have helps you build the confidence to successfully travel by yourself.

Tuning into your senses

To enjoy every moment without feeling overwhelmed by anxieties and concerns, you can also tune into your five senses. Pay attention to your surroundings, like your house or neighbourhood. Consider the colours you see, the smells, the noise, and so on. If you truly listen to your environment, you'll notice aspects you've never even considered. This technique allows you to appreciate your surroundings and focus on what happens in the here and now. Approach each detail you notice with curiosity and be grateful for it.

There are many ways in which you can boost your self-confidence and prepare yourself for the unexpected. In the sections above, we discovered solo activities which allow you to reflect on yourself and become more self-aware of who you are outside your comfort zone. We also looked at strategies to trust your decision-making skills and make effective choices. Finally, we learnt how to handle unforeseen challenges. The one thing you must accept is that you can't control everything. Don't waste emotional energy on things you can't control. Concentrate on those you can control. However, if you prepare a plan B (or a plan C, D, E, etc.) and practise mindfulness, you navigate difficulties more easily.

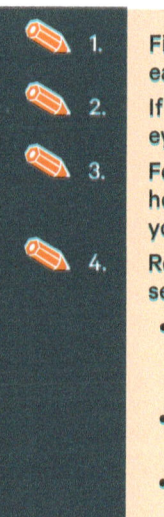
Darius Bashar - Unsplash

Remember, becoming comfortable with decision-making isn't just about big choices like solo travel but also the small day-to-day ones. Train your mind by making small decisions in your daily life to learn to trust your instincts.

In the previous chapter, we mentioned one common fear we all have when we venture on our own: loneliness. Fighting this negative feeling is not easy, but you can certainly do it. You'll learn more about it in the next chapter. ■

CHAPTER 3

Embracing solitude, not loneliness

Many people are trying to deal with loneliness and solitude when they're alone, but there's a profound difference between the two. Solitude is a choice, one where we intentionally seek time apart from others to engage in deep thinking and personal discovery. It's about finding peace in our own company and learning to grow from it. Therefore, we must learn to replace feelings of loneliness with appreciating solitude. This way, we understand ourselves better, thus improving self-awareness.

© Gordon Chesterman

In the next sections, we'll dive into the nuanced differences between loneliness and solitude, defining how recognising these distinctions can open up avenues for personal development and fulfilment. We will also examine how embracing solitude often leads to creative breakthroughs and heightened self-awareness. Additionally, we'll look at how solo travel serves as a practical framework to practise solitude. This chapter invites you to rethink your perceptions and provides guidance on how you can harness solitude.

Loneliness vs. solitude

Understanding the difference between loneliness and solitude is crucial in managing our emotions and discovering new aspects of ourselves. Loneliness is a feeling of emotional disconnection. It's often experienced when a person feels isolated, even if they're surrounded by others. This emotion may lead to negative impacts on mental health, causing feelings of depression or anxiety due to the perceived lack of social connection. If you feel lonely, you might feel like you're on the outside looking in, unable to bridge the gap which separates you from the world and those around you.

Solitude, on the other hand, is a conscious choice. It's an intentional state where you seek time away from others. Unlike loneliness, solitude is not associated with feelings of alienation. Instead, it offers a rich space for personal growth as it allows you to process thoughts without external influences. Many find that in solitude, creativity blossoms, and an inner dialogue strengthens, resulting in heightened self-awareness.

Feelings of loneliness are pretty common among solo travellers. For example, some people feel this way when travelling in bustling cities. Even if they're surrounded by lots of people, they still feel detached from the vibrant atmosphere and those populating it. These experiences explain the paradox of feeling alone amidst crowds, showing that loneliness is more a matter of emotional state than physical surroundings. Such travellers might describe their experiences of wandering through lively markets, hearing a cacophony of voices around them while feeling internally muted.

Renowned solo travellers have embraced solitude for centuries and seen it as a way of discovering themselves on a deeper level. Authors, musicians, and artists have often cited periods of solitude as

© Gordon Chesterman

I acknowledge the importance of solitude in my work and personal growth. In general, I don't use social media often and realise that I'm at my most creative when I'm alone in the quiet, so I enjoy spending time with myself. Sometimes, I might even spend many days in a row without leaving the house until I need to go to the supermarket to restock on food. I always find interesting things to do, from working on my personal and professional projects to playing the guitar, keyboards or watching YouTube videos. I thrive on solitude and don't tend to panic if I don't see or hear from my family and friends for some time. When I lived in Tenerife, I maybe saw my family once a year at Christmas until I actually moved back to the UK. Maybe being alone for extended periods might be too much for you at first, but you can still try to spend more time with yourself.

In addition to real stories, statistics highlight the increasing number of people seeking solitary adventures as a route to self-discovery. A remarkable rise in solo trips suggests more people now value this enriching experience. Especially interesting is the growing trend among women who embark on solo holidays, driven by a desire for freedom and the chance to explore the world on their own terms (Russell, 2023). Solo travel grants everyone the opportunity to step away from normal routine, societal roles and expectations, empowering them to embrace their true identities.

The benefits of such travel extend beyond immediate happiness, impacting aspects such as mental well-being and confidence. Travelling alone forces us to rely solely on personal judgement and decision-making abilities, enhancing both self-trust and problem-solving skills. When faced with challenges abroad, we learn resilience and adaptability—qualities which we can carry home to tackle everyday life. Adventures that once seemed daunting become sources of pride and accomplishment, reinforcing a positive relationship and belief in ourselves.

But solitude not only fosters self-reflection; it also nurtures a deepened understanding of our own desires and needs. During moments of quiet, we can evaluate what's important and truly fulfils us, thus feeling more satisfied in life. Moreover, solitude inspires creativity by offering unobstructed time to muse over ideas. Many famous figures attest to the power of these solitary moments, recounting how seclusion allowed them to push creative boundaries and realise hidden potential. The absence of external pressures provides the freedom to express our innate creativity.

Using loneliness to understand yourself

If you ever feel lonely during your travels, remember to see it as an opportunity to become more self-aware and improve yourself. The key to turning these seemingly daunting periods into enlightening experiences lies in recognising the emotional triggers which spark feelings of loneliness. A practical and effective method to achieve this understanding is through journalling.

fundamental times when they've created some of their finest work. These solitary journeys offer a sanctuary from daily distractions and provide the uninterrupted time for deep thinking and fostering great innovation. Imagine a writer retreating to a cabin in the woods, free from interruptions, finding that the peace and quiet unlocks new worlds within their stories.

I'm certainly not like the famous authors and artists of the past, but

CHAPTER 3

Journalling is like a mirror that reflects your innermost thoughts and feelings with clarity. When you travel alone, maintaining a journal allows you to document not just the external landscapes you encounter but also the internal journeys you undertake. If you record the emotions you experience during solitary moments, you can identify patterns which might otherwise remain hidden. For instance, noting what specific situations make you feel lonely—be it dining solo at a restaurant or venturing out in a new city—provides insights into your emotional landscape.

Inner reflection is always invaluable for detecting recurring themes in your personal feelings of loneliness and understanding how they impact your behaviour and mindset. If you want, you can start keeping a journal before travelling. Begin by dedicating a few minutes each day to reflect. Use prompts such as "What emotions did I feel most strongly today?" or "What triggered my feelings of loneliness?" to guide your entries.

Similarly, engaging in creative arts—whether it's painting, playing a musical instrument, or crafting—provides a non-verbal outlet for expressing your emotions. These creative pursuits often reveal subconscious feelings and allow you to process them safely and constructively. If creativity appeals to you, carry a small sketchbook or definitely a camera to capture your surroundings wherever you go to translate your experiences into artistic expressions.

Before starting on your solo travel, just try immersing yourself independently in activities that pique your interest. Whether it's visiting museums, hiking through nature trails, or attending local workshops, explore these interests to learn about who you are and what truly captivates you. You might even discover new passions and hobbies that enrich your life.

Ultimately, overcoming loneliness plays a crucial role in building your emotional resilience. If you embrace moments of solitude and confront feelings of loneliness head-on, you'll cultivate inner strength. By proving to yourself that you can navigate these periods of aloneness successfully, you gain confidence in your ability to tackle life's challenges. Emotional resilience grows through repeated exposure to difficult emotions and learning ways to manage them constructively. Each experience of overcoming loneliness adds a layer of depth to your emotional strength, preparing you to handle future situations.

Your character development is another positive outcome of using loneliness as a tool for deeper self-awareness. As you become more attuned to your emotional triggers and start addressing them, you begin to develop a richer, more nuanced understanding of yourself. This self-awareness fosters empathy and compassion not only for your own shortcomings but also for others. Recognising that loneliness is a shared human experience enables you to connect with people on a deeper level, as I'm hopefully doing with you in this book.

Balance connections with independence

As you might probably guess, an effective method to tackle solitude is to simply talk to others. When you travel alone, you'll likely interact with your friends and family at home, describing your journey and sharing details of the amazing experiences you have. However, if you want to make sure that you truly enjoy your travel and explore your inner self deeply, you must find a balance between communicating with loved ones and embracing solitude.

Let's take a look at some practical tips to achieve this. First, set clear expectations about how often you'll communicate with those back home. This can mean scheduling regular check-ins without letting technology take over your journey. By setting these boundaries, you ensure that you enjoy your experiences without constantly being tethered to your phone or laptop. You could decide on specific times or days for calls or messages, allowing both you and your loved ones to adapt to this new routine.

Tools such as video calls, messaging apps, and social media are excellent ways for maintaining regular updates. However, you should use them mindfully. For instance, you might send a quick photo or message every few days rather than engage in lengthy daily conversations. This approach provides peace of mind for those worried about your safety but allows you the freedom to immerse yourself in your adventures.

Besides, sharing travel stories and experiences upon return builds stronger relationships. When you're finally home, recounting your journey enriches your interactions. These stories foster a sense of closeness and offer insights into your growth and the new perspectives gained from your travels. You can share photographs, memorable moments, or cultural titbits to open up meaningful dialogue and appreciation with family and friends. Therefore, avoid spoiling everything along the road!

Staying in regular touch with loved ones is certainly important, but what about creating new connections? Engaging with locals or fellow travellers adds depth to your experience, offering new friendships which complement current relationships. Through casual encounters, attending local events, or participating in group activities, you develop a network that broadens your understanding. Conversations with people from diverse backgrounds also enable exchanges of ideas, thus helping you see things from different perspectives. But we'll look at how to build new connections in-depth in the next chapters.

Ultimately, embracing solitude while staying connected requires thoughtful planning and execution. The steps just outlined will help you maintain harmonious relationships while pursuing your goals. As you integrate these practises, you'll find that the balance between solitude and connection improves not only your travel experiences but all aspects of life.

Now you know the difference between loneliness and solitude. While loneliness might make you feel disconnected from those around you, even in a crowd, solitude is a personal choice that offers a chance for self-reflection and creativity. By diving into activities such as journalling, meditation, or creative arts during these solitary moments, you transform feelings of loneliness into opportunities for deeper self-awareness and fulfilment. At the same time, remember to balance solitude with experiences of connection. It's about finding that sweet spot between spending time alone and building meaningful relationships, both old and new.

After dealing with feelings of loneliness and solitude, it's time to explore practical ways to mentally prepare for the unknown. ■

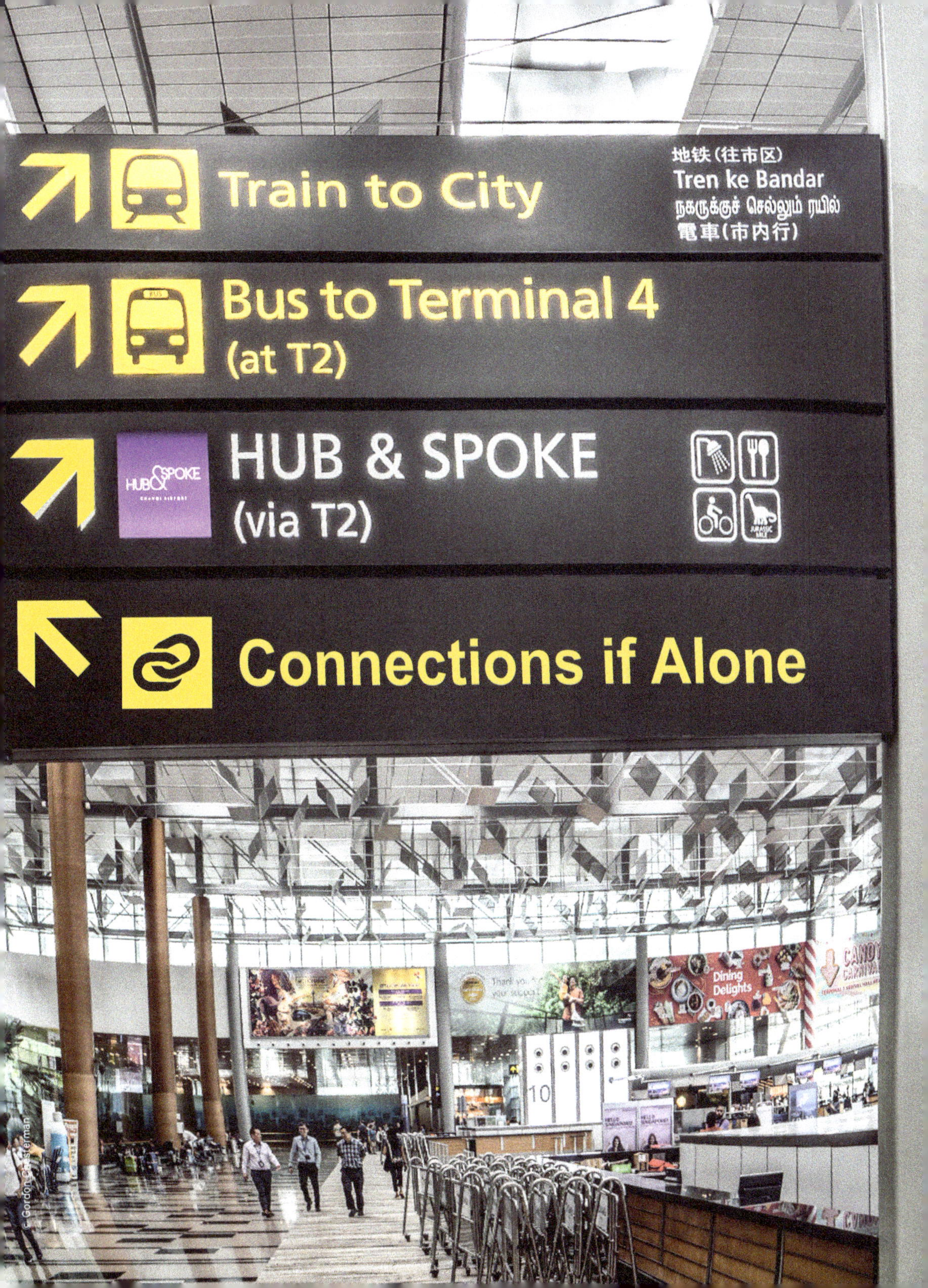

↗ 🚈 Train to City 地铁(往市区)
　　　　　　　　　　Tren ke Bandar
　　　　　　　　　　நகருக்குச் செல்லும் ரயில்
　　　　　　　　　　電車(市内行)

↗ 🚌 Bus to Terminal 4
　　　(at T2)

↗ HUB & SPOKE
　　(via T2)

↖ Connections if Alone

CHAPTER 4

Mentally preparing for your journey

Obviously, packing everything you need, booking the flight ticket, and all that stuff is essential to prepare yourself effectively. But first, you need to be mentally prepared. Before setting out on your adventure, mentally gearing up can make all the difference in transforming a potential experience from overwhelming to exciting. It's all about opening yourself up to the spirit of exploration while overcoming those internal whispers of doubt and hesitation.

First, we'll dive into the nuts and bolts of building mental resilience for your upcoming travels. You'll learn why it's beneficial to start small, gradually opening yourself up to new situations until comfort transforms into excitement. As you gain confidence, we'll look at ways to take on and tackle bigger goals, encouraging you to take on experiences you thought beyond your reach. By setting manageable targets, you'll see the growth and empowerment that comes with each step outside your comfort zone.

Opening up gradually

To build up mental resilience and shift toward embracing adventure, you need to start by gradually opening yourself up to brand new experiences. This way, you foster flexibility and build the resilience needed to tackle larger challenges.

The idea of gradually opening up comes from exposure therapy, which involves confronting fears one step at a time.

The key is starting small. Short trips or day outings are excellent ways to begin acclimatising to unfamiliar surroundings without feeling overwhelmed. For instance, consider visiting a nearby attraction or town. These short soirées help you become comfortable with being alone in new settings and provide an opportunity to understand your own responses and adapt accordingly. These experiences not only break the monotony but also instil a sense of accomplishment, knowing you successfully ventured beyond your comfort zone.

As you build confidence through these smaller ventures, it becomes essential to progressively take on more challenging experiences. Gradual exposure to increasingly demanding situations enhances your ability to cope and grow. This could mean taking longer trips, trying adventure activities such as hiking or kayaking, or even travelling to culturally diverse regions. These experiences accumulate to foster a robust self-image and a sense of real achievement, encouraging further exploration and personal development.

© Gordon Chesterman

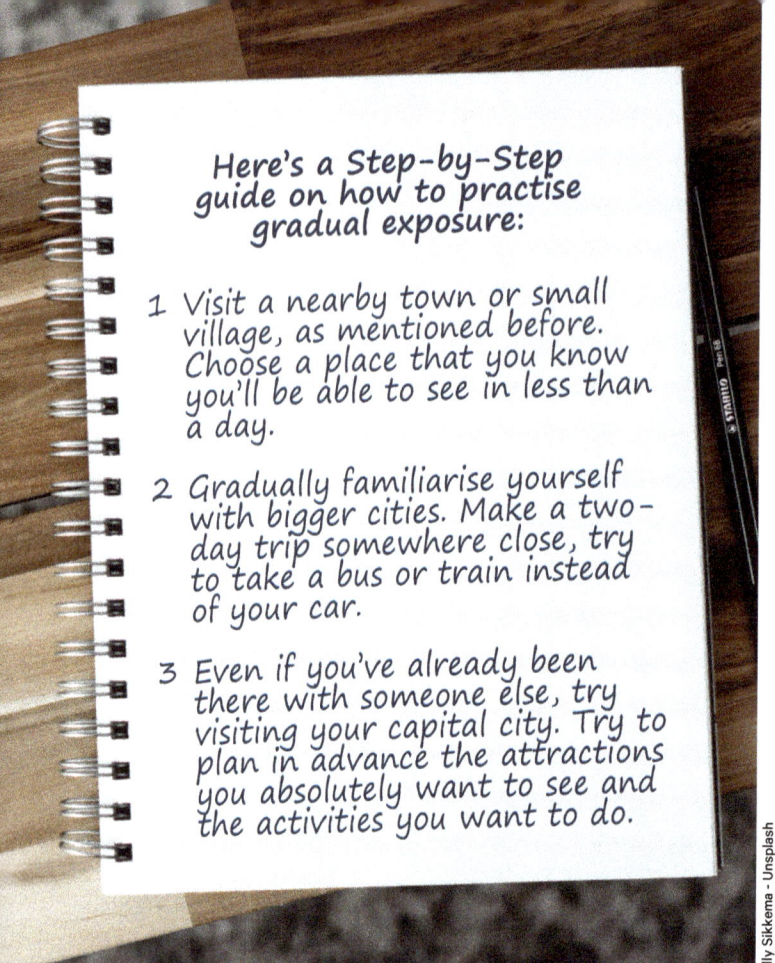

Here's a Step-by-Step guide on how to practise gradual exposure:

1. Visit a nearby town or small village, as mentioned before. Choose a place that you know you'll be able to see in less than a day.

2. Gradually familiarise yourself with bigger cities. Make a two-day trip somewhere close, try to take a bus or train instead of your car.

3. Even if you've already been there with someone else, try visiting your capital city. Try to plan in advance the attractions you absolutely want to see and the activities you want to do.

Kelly Sikkema - Unsplash

You don't have to follow the above steps to the letter, and you don't need to take all of them in a few weeks. Take your time to familiarise yourself with new surroundings and be patient with yourself. Remember, it's not about rushing head first into discomfort but gently expanding your boundaries. Each successful outing reinforces your capability to handle unfamiliarity, thus making future travels less intimidating and more enjoyable.

If you need help organising trips for two or three days, you can simply search online. For instance, I found TravelZoo to be quite useful. Sites like this can make it easy to book a short stay and plan what to do. These little trips are great for practising the processes and routines of going on a small break by yourself.

Set personal goals

Gradual exposure doesn't help much if you don't set clear goals. When you plan to make longer trips, you must be aware of the objectives you want to reach and why you do what you do. In order to make the most of your solo travel, it's essential to create a purpose-driven experience. This approach guides your journey and infuses each step with intention and meaning.

Let's start with defining your motivations. Understanding why you want to explore the world by yourself is a powerful tool for enriching your travels. Is it to escape your daily routine and discover new cultures, or perhaps to challenge your comfort zone and grow from overcoming fears? Defining these motivations will help shape your decisions and intentions along the way. By having a clear picture of what drives you, you can focus on the activities and destinations that align with these desires, ensuring a more fulfilling travel experience.

Once you've identified your key motivations, establish some achievement milestones to sustain your inspiration. These milestones will act as a road map, providing direction and measurable goals to work toward. For instance, if you're eager to immerse yourself in local cultures, a milestone could be learning basic phrases of the local language or participating in local festivals. As you achieve each milestone, not only do you get a sense of accomplishment, but it also helps maintain momentum. When setting these targets, consider creating a realistic timeline which encompasses all stages of planning, saving, and executing your trip, helping to ensure everyday tasks don't overshadow your long-term aspirations.

To keep track of your progress, you can share your goals with someone you trust. If you openly discuss your objectives with other people, they become more real, and you feel more motivated and dedicated to reaching them. At the same time, when others know about your intentions, they can provide essential support and accountability. The shared enthusiasm from those close to you can become an inspirational force that propels you forward. You might find encouragement in moments of doubt and celebration during successes, strengthening your resolve to keep pursuing your travel dreams.

Visualise success

Back in Chapter 1, we mentioned the visualisation technique to challenge your fears before leaving for your journey. Now, we'll explore these practises further to help you prepare mentally and increase positive feelings associated with your travel.

Creating a 'vision board' can be a powerful method to channel your travel aspirations into tangible forms. This tool serves as a daily reminder of what excites you about your adventure. Gather images and words that resonate with your goals—whether it's a serene beach in Thailand or a bustling market in Morocco. Arrange these elements in a collage that speaks to your inner wanderer. Hang this vision board somewhere visible, such as above your desk or near your bed, ensuring that each day, you are inspired by the destinations and experiences you long to explore.

Moreover, integrate positive affirmations into your routine to reshape your mindset toward travel. Affirmations are short, positive statements that combat negative beliefs, reframing them into empowering truths. Write these messages in the present tense, focusing on phrases like "I am capable of navigating new places"

or "I embrace all the adventures my travels bring." Regularly repeating these affirmations will foster a supportive internal dialogue and transforms your anxiety into excitement and anticipation. By reinforcing positive thoughts, you lay the groundwork for a journey filled with growth and happiness.

Visualisation does not end with crafting physical boards or verbal mantras; it extends into imagining successful scenarios. Close your eyes and picture yourself smoothly

© Gordon Chesterman

transitioning from one aspect of your trip to another. Envision arriving calmly at a foreign airport, efficiently handling your luggage, and confidently interacting with locals. Vividly imagine these scenes, engaging all your senses. Smell the aroma of local cuisine, hear the foreign chatter around you, and feel the texture of cobblestones underfoot. This exercise helps you build mental familiarity with positive outcomes, enhancing your confidence when encountering such situations in reality.

Visualising positive outcomes once is not enough to build your confidence. If you want to try the above activities, do it consistently

in your daily routine. Dedicate a few minutes every day to looking at your vision board and revisiting it or repeating positive affirmations. As these practises become habitual, observe how your perceptions change. You may notice less apprehension and a heightened level of excitement at the prospect of exploring new cultures and places.

We have explored how to build your mental resilience and shift your mindset toward embracing adventure. By starting small with solo day trips or local activities, you can gradually build determination and adaptability. As you gain confidence from smaller ventures, take on bigger challenges, such as longer trips and culturally diverse experiences. This gradual exposure enhances your ability to cope with uncertainties and fosters personal growth. Remember to be patient with yourself and take all the time you need to gradually familiarise yourself with new settings.

To sum up, go on as many local trips as you need to confirm you're mentally prepared. If you are, you can take the next step of planning a trip abroad. ∎

CHAPTER 5

Crafting your perfect itinerary

Now comes the really big test of planning your trip abroad. Crafting your perfect itinerary is a task that combines the art of planning with the freedom of flexibility. It involves building a road map tailored to your unique tastes and comforts, ensuring a balance between what you want to see and the spontaneous discoveries along the journey. Structuring a journey which caters to your interests while allowing room for unplanned adventures creates an enriching experience which unfolds at your own pace.

Throughout this chapter, you'll learn how to prepare practically and choose destinations that not only spark your interest but also meet your safety needs. Dive into the specifics of gathering valuable information from diverse sources and understand how to incorporate downtime for reflection and rest. You'll discover practical insights on how to balance structure with spontaneity—all aimed at making your holiday as enjoyable and fulfilling as possible. By the end, you'll have a comprehensive guide to help you navigate the complexities of independent travel, allowing you to embrace new experiences with confidence and ease.

Select the right destination

First things first, you must choose the right travel destination. It all starts with understanding what truly excites you. Identifying your personal interests not only helps in selecting destinations but also enhances your overall travel experience. Whether you're passionate about art, enjoy the tranquillity of nature, or thrive on adventure sports, aligning your interests with your travel plans creates memorable and fulfilling journeys. In addition to thinking about your interests, consider what you like about a place. Do you prefer hot or cold weather? Are you more comfortable in big cities or small villages? Do you like spending time on the beach or prefer the mountains? Are you looking for a real adventure in the wild or to do some sightseeing in renowned cities?

Let's say you're an art enthusiast; visiting places known for their art museums and vibrant street art scenes should be high on your list. Imagine wandering through the halls of the Louvre in Paris, the architecture of Rome or exploring the eclectic street art of Berlin. Each location brings a different flavour and culture, allowing you to dive deep into what you love while experiencing something new. For nature lovers, serene landscapes such as the majestic fjords in Norway or the lush rice terraces in Bali might call to you. Each destination offers unique experiences that resonate with what makes you tick.

Talking about safety

No matter how compelling your chosen destination may seem, safety must remain the top priority. Researching the safety conditions of potential destinations is crucial. Begin by familiarising yourself with local laws, because customs and legalities may differ vastly from what you're used to at home. Understanding cultural norms also prevents misunderstandings and helps you show respect to the locals and their traditions.

Singapore have strict laws regarding the following:

- **Drugs:** Having drugs in your system is illegal, and penalties range from caning to the death sentence for some trafficking offences.
- **Public behaviour:** It's illegal to be drunk and undisciplined in public.
- **Alcohol:** You're not allowed to drink in public between 10:30p.m. and 7a.m.
- **Chewing gum:** You can't import or sell chewing gum. If caught consuming it, you may be fined at least S$500.
- **Overstaying your visa:** Tourists face a fine up to S$4,000 or imprisonment up to six months if they stay in Singapore for more than 90 days without permission.
- **Jaywalking:** You're not allowed to cross roads erratically outside of designated places.

© Singapore Police Force

For your own safety, it's also wise to really delve deeper into current travel advisories and health considerations. Use online resources such as government websites or health organisations to stay informed about any travel warnings or required vaccinations. For example, I live in the UK, so I visit www.gov.uk/foreign-travel-advice which lists 226 countries. You simply click on the country you're interested in for the latest news and travel info. The World Health Organization (WHO) also provides valuable insights, such as health risks and necessary precautions when travelling to specific countries.

After assessing the basic safety conditions, consult travel reviews for real-life perspectives. These reviews often come from fellow travellers who share authentic experiences and tips. Platforms such as TripAdvisor or travel blogs give you a sense of what to expect at your chosen destination. Beyond general overviews, look for mentions of safety experiences, which might highlight areas to avoid or advice on navigating local transportation safely. While reviews are helpful, remember to apply a critical eye, cross-checking information across multiple sources to paint the clearest picture possible. In the end, it's normal people who write reviews and they may express a subjective view.

An essential tool in ensuring a safe and enjoyable trip is creating a customised safety checklist for your destination. List emergency contacts such as local embassies and healthcare facilities. Check if your mobile phone will work abroad, or consider getting a local SIM card to ensure you're reachable. It's also important to note down local emergency numbers since they differ from country to country. This checklist acts as your guide to staying prepared for unforeseen situations.

To further enhance personal safety, consider geopolitical climate and crime rates of your destination. https://travelaware.campaign.gov.uk/ offer detailed travel advisories, rating countries on safety levels ranging from exercising normal precautions to avoiding travel altogether due to severe security threats or political unrest. Understanding the level of risk helps you make informed decisions about where to go and how to behave once there.

As you're planning for your first solo trip, you should consider places that are generally considered safe. Perhaps choose a destination which is known for their welcoming culture or peaceful environments, such as Singapore, Japan or New Zealand, all celebrated for their hospitality and low crime rates.

In my case, visiting Singapore was the best decision I could make. This is because, as you just learnt, Singapore can have harsh penalties, therefore, people abide by the rules and are very respectful. For example, you can leave your bag on a table to reserve your seat at any Hawker food centre in the city while you go to choose your order without worrying about it. Personally, I didn't do this. I never let my cameras out of my sight. During my stay, I often saw young girls and women jogging on their own at 1 or 2 o'clock in the morning. You probably won't see such activity in other large cities!

I felt very safe wandering around the city with my cameras around my neck. In other countries, I've sensed being eyed as a mugging target by groups of young lads. But in Singapore, I think people only saw me as a professional photographer and were even sometimes curious to know more. Once, I even left my room safe open with my laptop, passport, and money in full view. When I came back, the cleaner had shut the safe door and closed the drawer it was in. Safety is just one of the many reasons why I would recommend Singapore as a first destination to try out everything you learn in this book.

In addition to following the aforementioned tips to ensure you stay safe, you can use helpful apps depending on your situation and requirements. Some popular ones are:

Searching 'Best personal safety Apps' on Google will list a lot results so you can investigate which will be best for your own situation.

Practical preparations before departure

The more you prepare before leaving, the less anxious you'll feel when reaching your destination. Just keep in mind that you can't predict everything, and you may well encounter one or two unexpected challenges along the way.

© Gordon Chesterman

The first step after choosing your destination involves organising travel documents. This simple yet effective strategy will significantly reduce any stress during your journey. Begin by looking online for information about the required documents. Pay attention to the websites and ensure they're secure, accurate, and official. In general, you should look at government websites. If you're not sure whether it's official or not, just ask Google (others have probably had the same doubts). This is particularly helpful if you go to areas such as Southeast Asia where information online might not be as clear and detailed as in other places.

After checking all the documents you need, write them down and start preparing them.

In general, you will need:

- Passport (make sure it's current and valid well past the date of your proposed return)
- Visa (if required)
- Travel insurance
- Itinerary
- International driver's licence (if driving whilst there)
- Accommodation reservations
- Vaccination certificates (if needed)
- Emergency contacts information
- Credit cards
- Transportation tickets
- Any necessary permits or tickets for activities

Store these documents in a dedicated travel wallet or folder, making them easily accessible when needed. Ensure you make photocopies or digital scans of these documents as backups. Having your paperwork in order helps you feel more in control and reduces the likelihood of any surprise stressors that could disrupt your travel plans.

I know a little bit about this. When catching a flight in Tenerife airport, I used a transparent plastic sleeve to keep my passport and flight tickets. Trying to be mega-efficient, I took out the plastic sleeve whilst walking the length of the airport to the check-in desk. However, I wasn't aware that it opened at the top *and* the side. The result was my passport dropped out, and I didn't notice until I got to the check-in desk. I retraced my steps but no passport. This resulted in more or less emptying all my bags on the airport floor. Still no passport. Then I went to the airport police office and explained the situation. The officer took my passport from his desk, checked my photo, and handed it over with a smile. Funnily enough, he was also the officer checking the passports at my boarding gate, so we had a little laugh about it as I thanked him once again.

This experience taught me two important things: -

Rule One:
Keep the sleeve or folder of tickets and docs in your carry-on bag at all times until the exact moment you actually need them.

Rule Two:
Don't break Rule One.

CHAPTER 5

With all your essential documents, prepared, research your destination. Familiarise yourself with cultural norms, customs, and transport options to boost your confidence and ease your lingering anxieties. Use guidebooks, reputable travel websites, forums, and YouTube to gather information about the area you'll be visiting. For my Singapore trip, videos were invaluable. They provided tips, do's and don'ts, plus ideas of places to eat and visit. I watched them for about six months planning my itinerary.

Knowing basic phrases in the local language also enhances your interactions and helps you navigate unfamiliar environments more smoothly. But we'll look at that later on. Understanding how to use public transport or how much taxi fares should be, can prevent confusion and potential exploitation and/or basically getting ripped off. Being well-informed helps you anticipate challenges and makes the entire experience more enjoyable and seamless.

You don't need to see all this research as a chore, but as a fun activity you can do in your free time. Whenever you want, simply search online for things to do, see, avoid, and the pros and cons of visiting your destination. There are many YouTubers who describe their travels down to the smallest detail and provide valuable information about prices, cost of living, common scams, and much more.

Another important element that allows you to maintain peace of mind is establishing a personal travel routine. This way, you add comfort and structure amidst the unpredictability of travelling. Everyone has their own daily habits, so try to maintain some semblance of your regular routine even while on the road. Maybe you're used to having a cup of coffee in the morning, taking a nap in the afternoon, or reading a book before going to sleep. Integrating familiar practises into your schedule provides a sense of home normality. If you are travelling across time zones, gradually adjust your sleep schedule in advance to minimise jet lag. This is especially important if you travel eastbound, as the body usually takes more time to adjust to going to bed and waking up earlier. A regular routine serves as an anchor, helping to ground you and keep stress levels in check, especially when everything else around you may seem unfamiliar.

Pack Smart

Last but not least, pack strategically. Packing smartly boosts readiness, alleviates stress, and ensures emotional reassurance throughout your trip. Make a comprehensive list of essentials based on the climate and activities planned at your destination. Prioritise versatile clothing items which can be layered, saving space in your luggage. Consider investing in packing cubes to organise your belongings and make it easier to find things without cluttering your suitcase. Don't forget to pack a small first-aid kit and any medications you might need, along with important electronic chargers and adapters. Being prepared means you're less likely to face last-minute scrambles to find forgotten items, which can dampen your travel enthusiasm.

Here's a list of items everyone should *consider* keeping in their suitcase:

- Reusable water bottle
- Travel-sized toiletries
- Portable power bank
- Lightweight travel blanket or scarf for warmth or as a makeshift pillow
- Small notebook or journal
- Comfortable walking shoes
- Sun protection and sunglasses
- Compact umbrella or a poncho (in some places such as Singapore, an umbrella is vital for both unpredictable downpours and as a sun shade)
- Map or guidebook (if internet is unreliable)
- Any specific gear or equipment needed for planned activities such as hiking boots etc.
- Backup credit/debit cards (keep separate from primary ones just in case)
- Lightweight bag for day trips and excursions
- A small stash of medicine for common ailments, pain relief, digestion aids, or allergies
- Camera or smartphone
- Essential items from home that provide comfort
- Power adapter suited to the destination
- Lightweight raincoat or windbreaker
- Travel neck pillow

PixelShot - AdobeStock

CHAPTER 5

In addition to these organisational strategies, practising relaxation techniques also helps manage pre-travel jitters. Engage in slow breathing exercises or download relaxation apps to calm your nerves. Incorporating physical activity into your pre-travel preparations, such as going for a walk or doing yoga, releases endorphins that naturally reduce stress. Remember, taking care of your mental health is just as critical as planning the logistical aspects of your trip.

Gather information from different sources

The internet is an invaluable tool that allows you to research anything you want, from tips to stay safe to the best travel destinations in the world. However, everyone can write whatever they want online. **So, be diligent and choose your sources carefully.** It's important to tap into a variety of resources which offer comprehensive insights and make your trip smooth and enjoyable. Don't limit yourself to looking at one online blog, but explore each topic in detail and ensure different people agree and provide the same information.

One of the best ways to do this is by using travel apps and websites that provide real-time information on itineraries and destinations. These tools help you organise your travel plans, especially when you're navigating unfamiliar places alone. Apps like Google Maps are indispensable for directions and understanding public transport options, while hotel booking sites such as Booking.com or Airbnb help you find accommodation that fit both your budget and personal preference. By using worldwide-known websites, you ease concerns about security and safety. You wouldn't want to find yourself in the middle of nowhere or book a hotel to discover it's a homestay, would you?

For example, I researched my hotel in Singapore by looking it up on Trustpilot. Any decent place will have reviews on this site, and they're up to date. Even after reading them, I still had questions, so I contacted the hotel directly by email on two occasions. They replied within a few hours, and their answers were reassuring.

Using travel apps and websites efficiently involves knowing which ones will serve you best based on your specific needs. If you're concerned with budget, apps such as Skyscanner or Hopper track flight prices and alert you to the best deals. For those who love planning every detail, VisitACity offers tailored itineraries based on how many days you'll be in your various destinations, giving you suggestions on what to do each day while leaving room for discovery and spontaneity. Just ask Google, and you'll find numerous websites and apps.

Another handy tool in your solo travel toolkit should be online travel communities. Joining forums or social media groups dedicated to travel connects you with travellers who share firsthand experiences and valuable tips. These communities often provide support through practical advice on what attractions to visit, which activities are worth your time, and even warnings about tourist traps to avoid. This peer-to-peer interaction also helps soothe any nervousness about travelling

alone, as you realise others have had similar worries but managed to overcome them successfully.

Useful communities such as Reddit (*r/solotravel* in particular), Quora, or Facebook connect you with seasoned globetrotters and fellow solo adventurers. It's here that you can ask questions, share plans, or just read about others' experiences. You'll find people willing to offer tips about

The Buddha Tooth Relic Temple

Respect Customs

packing, safety advice, or even recommendations on must-see places which you might not find on the usual travel lists. This communal learning might boost your confidence, knowing there's a network of support out there, even if they're only virtual.

While digital resources are fantastic, don't overlook the value of consulting local experts once you arrive at your destination. Hotel staff, tour guides, or even friendly locals can offer insider knowledge which isn't available online. Nothing beats having a conversation with someone who calls the place home. So, approach hotel concierges or hosts for reliable dining recommendations or safe neighbourhoods to explore. Local tour guides, often passionate about their hometown, can give you a taste of authenticity that the internet can't always convey. These interactions may lead you to uncover stories, history, and places that typical tourists might miss out on, transforming your trip into a series of amazing discoveries.

In addition to seeking expert advice, research the cultural norms of the places you plan to visit. Understanding local customs, traditions, and etiquette prevents misunderstandings (most of the time) and fosters a more immersive travel experience. For example, knowing whether it's customary to tip service staff, appropriate attire for religious sites, or even basic phrases in the local language goes a long way in making connections with the people you meet along your journey. Not only does this show respect for the culture, but it also enriches your travel narrative.

Incorporate downtime for rest and reflection

If you're very excited about your solo travel like many others, you may look for all the things to do and see once there and make a list. A long list. Without realising it, you might plan every second of your day there and leave no time for some rest. The excitement and craving for exploration are understandable, but it's also important to incorporate some downtime to just relax and check in with yourself.

Planning relaxation time into your schedule counterbalances the inevitable hustle and bustle of travel, thus reducing fatigue and allowing you to recharge. Travel can often feel like a marathon, especially if you're trying to see and do as much as possible. However, this constant movement without taking a break might quickly lead to exhaustion, reducing the fun of discovering new places. By deliberately setting aside time for relaxation, you're essentially giving yourself permission to slow down and soak in the atmosphere at your own pace. Imagine reclining under a café umbrella in a sun-dappled square, simply watching the world go by, or lounging on a grassy bank beside a river, book in hand.

city's history or culture, provide just the right balance of learning and leisure. They're an excellent way to gather insights while allowing yourself to absorb the environment slowly and thoroughly. When you're travelling alone, walking tours can also offer social interaction without the pressure of committing to group events, making them an ideal match.

Travel has such a wonderful way of pushing us out of our comfort zones, but it's vital to pay attention to our physical and emotional needs. This means being attuned to signs of fatigue, stress, or burnout and

won't be able to walk at your usual pace. When I was in Singapore, I noticed locals walking quite slowly and eventually understood why. If I had walked at my normal speed, I would have probably passed out with the humidity!

Solo travel is an opportunity for personal growth and self-discovery. On the one hand, it's about embracing new places; on the other, it's about understanding yourself better. Allocating time for rest and reflection facilitates this dual-purpose journey, turning visual snapshots into meaningful

Always remember to take time out

© Gordon Chesterman

Moreover, consider taking short naps, indulging in a spa session, or practising some relaxation techniques to unwind and recover after a day of exploration.

Walking tours or casual strolls through local parks offer leisurely exploration while keeping things light and relaxed. Unlike high-intensity activities that may drain energy reserves, these options provide gentle exercise, promote curiosity, and invite spontaneous discovery without overwhelming you. Walking tours, which often feature knowledgeable guides sharing interesting tales about a

adjusting your plans accordingly. Maybe a particular day calls for fewer activities, or maybe it's time to swap that crowded tourist attraction for a quiet afternoon at a local bookstore. Recognising when to slow down or modify plans ensures the experience remains pleasant rather than becoming a route march. If you adopt this mindset, you maintain a healthy balance that prioritises well-being and personal satisfaction over rigid adherence to a 'must do' schedule.

For instance, consider the climate of your destination. If it's particularly hot and humid there, you probably

life chapters. By integrating rest periods into your itinerary, you allow space for both adventure and introspection.

Balancing structure and spontaneity

Similar to downtime, spontaneity is important in every travel. Pre-planning all the activities you want to do doesn't allow you to enjoy the moment and maybe take a few opportunities that arise out of nowhere. By balancing structure and spontaneity, you enhance your travel experience and make it more flexible.

CHAPTER 5

How can you find the perfect balance? Start by outlining the essential activities which align with your interests and must-see attractions. These are the experiences you've been dreaming about—whether it's visiting a specific historical site, attending a local event, or trying out renowned cuisine. Listing these in advance ensures you won't miss out on key experiences during your trip.

In fact, while it's important to include essential activities, it's good to leave some time unplanned. You should set aside parts of your day where you don't have any plans so that you have the freedom to wander and explore at your own pace.

Unplanned excursions may become the highlight of your trip. By encouraging yourself to wander without a definite plan, you open up the possibility of discovering hidden gems that weren't featured in any travel guide or pre-trip research. It could be a charming café, a picturesque street, or a local festival you stumble upon. Embracing these unplanned adventures adds a layer of excitement and authenticity to your journey and makes each day unpredictable and enjoyable.

To facilitate this blend of planned and spontaneous activities, you can use a "loose" itinerary format.

── My Must-See List ──

1. Visit my clients Xia Haiying and Koh Kai Mui, directors of City Ballet Academy. I designed their logo for the Singapore International Ballet Grand Prix.
Being in the UK, I worked remotely therefore, meeting them in person and saying hello, was a primary reason for going to Singapore.

2. Attend the Singapore Airshow which is held every two years. I booked the digital tickets in advance to avoid any stress of getting them on the day.

3. The Kranji War Cemetery. Being raised on RAF bases, it was a humbling experience and a place to reflect and appreciate the sacrifice which allowed me to be there.

4. Visit the houses I used to live in with my family as a 5-7 year old when we were 'posted' to RAF Changi.

I decided not to put too many items on my list. I wanted to be 100% sure I could complete them in the time I had. Crossing them off felt great and allowed me to relax and enjoy the other days as I wanted - without any stress.

45

> **Be flexible to go where your mood takes you**

Unlike conventional itineraries which dictate every step, a loose format provides a framework that guides you through your day while leaving room for changes. This approach might involve booking certain attractions or accommodation in advance but remaining flexible about when to visit them. For instance, if you plan to tour a museum but wake up feeling more inclined to relax at a park, a loose itinerary allows the flexibility to swap activities without any stress. Alternatively, choose an activity you absolutely want to do most on your trip and keep the rest of your plans open for spontaneity and relaxation.

You shouldn't see spontaneity as a way to sacrifice structure; rather, it's about finding a middle ground where you feel comfortable pursuing planned objectives while staying open to free exploration. When designing your itinerary, think of it as a living document rather than a fixed schedule. Life on the road can bring unexpected changes, so embrace an adaptable mindset to respond flexibly to unforeseen circumstances such as weather shifts or attraction closures. This adaptability lets you prioritise experiences based on your mood and energy levels each day. Feeling adventurous? Opt for a hike or explore an unfamiliar neighbourhood. Prefer a quieter day? Spend a leisurely afternoon in a cosy café, stroll through a serene park or laze on a beach.

When crafting your itinerary, remember that simplicity and enjoyment should be at the forefront. If you tend to feel anxious, sticking to strict plans might make you feel overwhelmed and worried. You feel like you need to follow your plan to the letter and do everything. On the contrary, if you have a loose itinerary, you will feel more relaxed. Knowing when to switch gears and spend quality downtime is as important as tackling sightseeing adventures. The trick lies principally in pacing yourself, and therefore fulfilling your desires while providing ample opportunities for unplanned activities.

The perfect solo travel itinerary is all about finding that sweet spot between planning and improvisation. Aligning your travel destinations with personal interests elevates your journey and adds richness to every step you take. However, safety is important too. A solid mix of thorough research and firsthand advice from online communities or locals paves the way for well informed decisions. In addition, don't forget those much-needed moments of rest and reflection, which are essential for keeping your travels pleasant. It's in the unexpected moments, the little adventures found off the beaten path, where you often find the most happiness. Dive into each moment with curiosity and embrace the balance of structure and spontaneity.

However, there are certainly two aspects of your travel where you need to plan: accommodation and transportation. Travel logistics might be a hurdle, but you can manage them effectively if you apply some useful strategies. ■

Marina Bay Sands

CHAPTER 6

Mastering travel logistics

Whether it's booking the perfect spot to lay your head or navigating local transportation, understanding these logistical elements will transform your travel into a smooth operation instead of a series of possible stressful events. With proper planning, everyone can find freedom and happiness in exploring the world at their own pace, confident in the knowledge that they've factored in everything.

First, we'll delve into the nitty-gritty details that make solo travel not only manageable but enjoyable. From choosing accommodation that fits both your budget and comfort needs to efficiently using public transport systems, you'll find tips tailored to ease your journey. Next, you'll discover how to confidently handle airport procedures, ensuring a stress-free start to your trip. You'll also learn about making flexible accommodation bookings, which will help you adapt with ease if and when plans change unexpectedly.

Choose the right accommodation

Choosing the perfect place to stay is a critical step toward a comfortable and stress-free trip. In fact, understanding your options significantly eases the anxiety associated with solo travel. The world of accommodation offers a variety of choices, including hotels, hostels, and short-term rentals, each with its own set of advantages. Choosing the right type depends largely on your personal comfort level and budget.

Hotels are often seen as the more traditional choice, offering a wide range of amenities such as room service, housekeeping, and sometimes even pools or gyms. They can give you a sense of security with their professional management and typically strong safety measures, such as 24-hour reception desks, which can be very reassuring if you're on your own. However, they might be more expensive compared to other types of accommodations.

The world of hostels are another option, particularly for those travelling alone who wish to meet new people. Many hostels offer both shared dormitories and private rooms, making them a flexible choice for various budgets. They're generally cheaper than hotels and can be a great way to connect with other travellers. However, the social setting of a hostel may not appeal to everyone, especially if you're an introvert looking for some peace and quiet or don't like being around a lot of people most of the time.

Short-term rentals found on platforms such as Airbnb offer a home-like experience and may provide better value if you're staying for longer periods. They often come with kitchen facilities, thus allowing you to cook your meals and save money. The privacy of having your own space can also be comforting for some, but it's important to thoroughly vet these places for safety before booking.

As always, safety should be a top priority. This means not only ensuring that the location itself has robust security measures in place—like secure locks, well-lit entrances, and possibly cameras—but also evaluating the neighbourhood it is in. Accommodation with 24-hour security or front desk service can

© Gordon Chesterman

add an extra layer of protection, allowing you to rest easy knowing there's someone available to help at any hour.

When you have to choose the right accommodation, use online reviews and ratings, which are invaluable tools in your decision-making process. Websites like TripAdvisor, Booking.com, and others allow past guests to share

their experiences, providing a window into what you can expect from a particular accommodation. Look for reviews that highlight aspects such as cleanliness, safety, location, and guest satisfaction. Pay special attention to comments about how the staff handles issues since their willingness to assist can greatly enhance your stay.

The strategic location is another crucial factor to consider. Staying somewhere with easy access to public transport and major attractions minimises logistical challenges, leaving you more time to enjoy your trip. When researching places to stay, check maps to gauge proximity to bus stations, subways, or key sites you plan to visit. A centrally located accommodation reduces travel time, lowers transport costs, and eliminates some of the stress linked with navigating unfamiliar areas.

That's exactly what I did. I looked at the map and chose a hotel in the centre of Clarke Quay—a stone's throw away from all the places I wanted to visit. I was lucky enough to find an excellent three-star hotel called The Quay Hotel with friendly staff, especially the receptionists. It's certainly on my radar the next time I go to Singapore.

When I finally booked my trip via Booking.com, I had to remember not to book the hotel for the day I was flying because the time difference meant I didn't need a bed for that night. I left on Wednesday morning and landed the next morning, so I needed a bed from Thursday night. Keep your flight arrival and time zones in mind when booking your accommodation. My experience with Booking.com was great, and I received a nice discount on my hotel price as a first-time user. Plus, the hotel was easy to contact through the app which I did a couple of times prior to my trip.

A good tip when booking hotels is to call them directly for prices. They'll be glad to have you as a "stocking filler," and you could get a discount for helping them occupy an otherwise empty room. Plus, you could get better prices than those offered on booking sites. How is this possible? There's a thing called a "parity clause," which is a sort of agreement between the hotel and booking site. The site agrees to list the hotel only if they don't advertise lower prices on their website. To get around this, hotels usually offer member-only discounts or better rates over the phone. So, call them! Even if you end up paying the same amount, the hotel might offer you a freebie, like free breakfasts. The best tactic to achieve this is by looking at hotels on known websites and checking their prices. Then, call them and ask them if there's a way to pay less than the advertised price.

In addition to booking sites, you can also look at comparison ones where you compare different prices to find the best deal. Just keep in mind that they don't check the quality of the websites they advertise, so choose carefully before booking.

There are lots of booking sites to choose from:

CHAPTER 6

Here's a few notable companies who cater for solo travellers:

Part of the fun of preparing is searching online for your own needs. Usually, the best search returns are from phrases such as "Best apps for…" or "Best websites for…"

If booking accommodation stresses you out, then why not remove that stress by simply going to your local travel agent? They'll be happy to help you—they're paid for it! Moreover, they may have offers and discounts which you might not know about or have access to.

Handle airport procedures with confidence

Airports provoke a peak in anxiety in all of us, especially if we're travelling alone. The hustle and bustle of terminals, the seemingly endless security lines, and the constant announcements can all contribute to feelings of overwhelm and stress. However, by understanding and preparing for each step of the airport process, you can ease these tensions and navigate your way with confidence.

The first step in making your airport experience smoother is breaking down the key procedures: check-in, security, and boarding. Familiarising yourself with these processes ahead of time drastically reduces stress levels, especially if you've never taken a flight before. You can check-in online or at self-service kiosks at the airport. If you check in online, you have the opportunity to choose your seat and print your boarding pass at home, cutting down on time spent waiting in line at the airport. Additionally, many airlines offer mobile boarding passes, which you can store on your phone for easy access.

Security is another major part of the airport experience. Generally, you'll need to remove shoes, belts, and any metal items before walking through security screening devices. Place your electronics in separate bins, as they typically require individual screening. If you're unfamiliar with the security process, consider watching videos online that show typical security checks. Keep in mind that although there are general guidelines which all airports adhere to, you may need to remove different items or follow different procedures. If you can't find any specific information online, the staff at the security check can help and tell you exactly what you need to do.

© Gordon Chesterman

Although security is usually very strict, it's not the same everywhere. When I visited Cape Verde islands, I flew from Sal to Boa Vista and was surprised by the security, or lack of. The check-in girl checked off passengers' names on a piece of paper. When the time came to weigh my bag, it was placed on one of those old scales people put money in to weigh themselves (maybe it was!). It was a quaint reminder of the good old days of flying. I felt like I was in a TV comedy sketch about seat of the pants travel.

The last step before you can finally relax in your seat is boarding the plane. It typically occurs in groups or zones, indicated on your boarding pass. Listen carefully for announcements or follow the digital displays near the gate for updates. Once it's your turn to board, have your identification and boarding pass ready to present to the gate agent.

One of the most important tips to follow is to arrive early at the airport. This is especially valid if you didn't do the check-in online and need to do it in person, which might mean facing long queues and delaying the moment you pass the security check. Arriving early also gives you ample time to navigate the terminal without rushing, allowing you to handle any unexpected incidents calmly (such as your passport dropping out of a plastic sleeve!). For domestic flights, aim to arrive at least two hours before departure; for international flights, three hours is better. This buffer not only reduces anxiety but also provides you with time to become familiar with the layout of the airport, find your gate, and explore any amenities available.

At the airport, your carry-on bag will become your life-saver, so pack it carefully. Keep important documents such as your passport, boarding pass, and any necessary visas accessible, ideally in a travel wallet or designated pocket. Additionally, include comforting items such as a book, earphones, or a neck pillow to make your journey more pleasant. Consider packing snacks and a bottle of water to stay nourished and hydrated before taking the flight. You'll probably need to spend some time at the airport, so it's better to have something to eat and drink with you. Once you pass the security check, you might not be able to keep snacks and water. However, if you take a long flight, they'll be provided to you by the staff onboard. In some cases, they're included in your flight ticket.

But what happens if there's a delay? Such situations can stress anyone out, especially if you have one or more layovers. These kinds

09:45	Dundee	LM622	Gate shown 09:00
09:50	Dublin	AC6907	Gate shown 09:00
09:55	Copenhagen	SQ2706	Gate shown 09:10
10:00	Shannon	AC6917	Gate shown 09:10
10:00	Vienna	OS454	Gate shown 09:20
10:05	Houston	SN9078	Gate shown 08:55
10:20	Stockholm	SQ2620	Gate shown 09:35
10:25	Warsaw	AI7762	Gate shown 09:40
10:25	Chicago	LH9348	Gate shown 09:15
10:30	Frankfurt	LH903	Gate shown 09:50
10:35	Oslo	SQ2660	Gate shown 09:50
10:55	Singapore	SK8037	Gate shown 09:45
1:00	Irl West Knock	EI915	Gate shown 10:10
1:05	Brussels	SQ2824	Gate shown 10:20
1:10	Mumbai	AC856	Gate shown 09:55
:10	Munich	LH2473	Gate shown 10:30
:20	Athens	A3601	Gate shown 10:35
30	Frankfurt	LH905	Gate shown 10:50
30	Istanbul	UA6919	Gate shown 10:45

CHAPTER 6

of interruptions are common, but having a plan in place prevents them from derailing your entire trip. Therefore, research the airports where you will have layovers to understand what facilities are available. Some larger airports offer lounge access, showers, or even small sleeping pods. Knowing what is available ahead of time allows you to decide how best to spend your time if delays occur. Bring in your carry-on bag things such as books, podcasts, or puzzles to keep your mind occupied and ward off boredom during waiting periods.

Little glitches can sometimes work out nicely. Due to ice, my flight from Manchester to Thailand was heavily delayed, therefore I missed all of my connections. Deboarding at Bangkok airport, I was thinking about what I needed to do when I was greeted by staff actually on the airbridge with my name on a board. After checking their authenticity they explained my rearranged flight wasn't until the next day, As a result, I was driven to stay at the Golden Tulip, a nice four star hotel in the centre of Bangkok. My overnight stay and evening meal was complimentary, plus I was chauffeur driven back to the airport to continue my journey.

The use of technology can simplify your travel experience, too. Flight tracking apps provide real-time updates on gates, departures, and arrivals, ensuring you're always informed. Many airports have their own apps which offer interactive maps and information about amenities, helping you find what you need quickly. Don't overlook the power of staying connected and informed. Joining airline loyalty programs or subscribing to their newsletters can give you valuable insights, such as exclusive offers, priority services, faster check-ins, or extra baggage allowances. Social media platforms and travel forums are also excellent resources for tips and advice from seasoned travellers who have encountered similar situations.

Use public transport safely and efficiently

After all that fatigue and time, you finally land! The next step is becoming familiar with local transit systems to grasp the basics and move around stress-free. If you've done your homework, you should know how public transportation works by now. This proactive step goes a long way in reducing the fear

Changi Airport App

BusRouter SG App

MRT App

of getting lost. You might start by researching online about the city's main transport options—do they have an efficient subway system, or are buses more commonly used? Understanding the routes and schedules helps piece together how you'll navigate from one point to another without unnecessary anxiety. Look for official transport websites, which often provide detailed maps and timetables. Moreover, these resources often highlight peak hours and less crowded times, thus giving you a sense of when it's best to travel.

If you can't find official websites, YouTube and Google can be extremely helpful. Look for online forums and videos about how to move around cities. This way, you can easily understand which types of transportation are better. For example, you may plan to travel around Asia by train but then discover that buses are more common, efficient, and cheaper.

Once you've absorbed the theoretical aspects, it's time to get tech-savvy. Leveraging maps and

© Gordon Chesterman

travel apps will make navigation smoother. Modern apps provide real-time updates about traffic conditions and any service changes, which means you can plan around delays and avoid unsafe situations that could arise, particularly late at night in unfamiliar areas.

© Gordon Chesterman

Download apps like Google Maps or Citymapper, which offer route suggestions based on current conditions—they're invaluable for keeping track of your journey, getting step-by-step directions, and even estimating costs. Some apps also offer offline capabilities, which are critical if your mobile data is limited while abroad. However, keep in mind that these apps might not be as accurate as you imagine. In some cases, they may not find the right address or might suggest an imprecise time frame to move from point A to point B. So, allow some flexibility in your journey and take possible delays into account.

When formulating your trip, consider travelling during the daylight hours. In fact, daylight provides not just visibility but also psychological comfort, thus reducing feelings of isolation which might come up when navigating public transport in an unfamiliar city. You can also think about travelling during peak times, which assures a higher flow of passengers and staff presence, contributing to a safer environment. Plus, public transport infrastructures generally operate more smoothly during these times, with fewer service disruptions. During these busy times, there's both safety in numbers and the chance to observe the locals to understand commute etiquette a little better. However, peak time is messy in all parts of the world. If you don't feel comfortable with making your way through crowds, think about taking public transportation a bit earlier or later.

Finally, it's also useful to actively engage with locals when appropriate. Many people love sharing tips about their hometown, and you might gain invaluable insights from those who use these systems daily. A simple gesture like asking for directions can open up conversations which lead to unexpected advice on little-known shortcuts or recommendations about places to visit. Engaging with locals also boosts your confidence as you realise there's a supportive community willing to help when needed. It's not just about asking questions; watching where locals queue, how they pay fares, or understanding unwritten rules is immensely helpful.

In Singapore, I learned about people's kindness. The only way to get around efficiently is using the mass rapid transport (MRT), so I had to try it. I was outside an MRT station and Google told me to enter the underground at "Entrance G," so I looked for it, but couldn't find it anywhere. There was every letter—just not the G. I simply froze with frustration. I was surrounded by people rushing by, minding their business and ignoring me as if I was invisible, It was work rush hour after all. However, it was clear I was having a problem. A woman walked close by, so I gently asked if she could point me in the right direction to the entrance I was looking for. I was surprised by her reply: It was clear she had to be somewhere herself, but she gladly helped me and provided very useful guidance. She even offered to accompany me back in to the

56

underground where she had just come from to take me to the right floor and platform. I thanked her for the offer but I was so embarrassed I couldn't navigate the most efficient and user friendly underground system in the world! However, it was so nice that she even considered it. In hindsight, I should have simply gone bacl down into the station and worked it out for myself.

Manage accommodation bookings when plans change

One of the most common aspects of travel that demands flexibility is accommodation bookings. Plans can change for numerous reasons—whether due to delayed flights, sudden health issues, or spontaneous decisions to change plans. Being prepared to adapt when these changes occur is invaluable, and mastering this adaptability begins with choosing the right booking options from the start.

For example, where possible, opt for accommodations with flexible cancellation or alteration policies to maintain peace of mind on the road. Many travel platforms now highlight properties offering lenient terms, allowing for cancellations or modifications without hefty penalties. My hotel in Singapore, The Quay Hotel, would refund the booking in full if I cancelled two days before. While these options might initially appear more expensive, they can save you both financial and emotional stress should plans go awry. However, it's crucial to understand the nuances of these policies, such as the timing required for a full refund versus a partial one. This way, you set realistic expectations and ensure you're not caught off guard by unexpected fees.

In addition to flexible bookings, protecting yourself with travel insurance acts as a valuable safety net in the face of uncertainties.

Insurance policies often cover issues like flight and trip cancellations, interruptions, or delays due to unforeseen events, reimbursing non-refundable costs. This financial safeguard allows for more organic and unplanned travel itineraries. If things don't go as planned, you won't be left footing a large bill. Select a policy that aligns with your travel habits and destinations while considering potential risks you might encounter on your journey.

Another key aspect of handling unexpected accommodation changes is having a backup plan. Consider alternative lodgings before starting your journey to reduce anxiety and equip you with pre-prepared solutions should your initial plans fall through. Researching nearby hotels, hostels, or Airbnb options ensures you're not left scrambling during a cancellation crisis. Make a note of their contact details and the distance in relation to your current location or points of interest. Then, check their availability regularly. By being proactive, you minimise disruption to your travel adventure and avoid wasting precious time on last-minute searches.

If you do need to alter your bookings, try to make sure to notify providers as soon as you can. A timely heads-up enhances your credibility with service providers and fosters a healthy relationship, which may lead to them being more accommodating to your needs. Transparent communication opens doors to find mutually beneficial alternatives. For example, if you inform your host about changes well in advance, they might offer a flexible adjustment, understanding that unforeseen circumstances are a part of travel life. Moreover, this transparency sometimes yields insider tips or support networks that can prove invaluable on your travels.

By following these tips, you not only simplify challenges but also become more confident in your skills. Learning to adapt improves your resilience and builds your ability to navigate other unpredictable elements of solo travel. In other words, it encourages a flexible mindset that allows you to face different challenges. Each adjustment is a step toward becoming a more seasoned traveller, one who is equipped to handle the ebbs and flows of exploration.

While travel logistics may be daunting for those new to solo travel, systematic preparations pave the way for successful trips. By implementing frameworks that prioritise safety, flexibility, and communication, each logistical hurdle becomes manageable. Such approaches transform the seemingly chaotic nature of travel into a structured journey, allowing you to revel in the freedom and independence that come with venturing into the world alone.

This chapter has walked you through choosing accommodation that fits your needs and budget, whether it's a hotel for comfort, a hostel for socialising, or a short-term rental for a home-like feel. Remember, safety should always be at the top of your mind. Look at online reviews and aim for places close to public transit and the attractions you want to explore. The chapter also delved into understanding local transport systems pre-trip, using apps for navigation, and engaging with locals as strategies to ease your journey. By mastering these practical aspects, you'll feel more in control and ready to embrace your adventures.

We've also touched on airport procedures, handling flights with confidence, and managing accommodation bookings with flexibility. Planning ahead and using tech tools streamlines your airport experience, while flexible booking options and travel insurance are key to adapting when plans change. Equip yourself with backup lodging choices and keep communication clear if changes arise—these small steps build resilience and make travelling less intimidating. Whether it's navigating an unfamiliar city or being prepared for flight delays, following these tips will turn potential obstacles into opportunities for growth.

Staying safe during your travel involves more than preparing for possible obstacles, unexpected events, and changes in plans. It also means taking care of your health and ensuring you know what to do if you feel sick. ■

© Gordon Chesterman

Natural Beauty

CHAPTER 7
Health and wellness abroad

The joy and thrill of discovering new places often comes with unpredictable changes in routine, making it crucial to maintain your well-being. Balancing physical wellness alongside mental peace forms the basis of any enjoyable experience when travelling alone. Imagine setting foot in uncharted lands with the confidence that you're prepared for any eventuality. Whether it's adjusting to a different climate or handling emergencies, understanding how to care for yourself ensures these adventures are as enriching as possible.

In this chapter, we look into practical strategies to keep healthy while travelling alone. You'll find guidance on sustaining daily habits which promote wellness even when you're far from home. From choosing nutritious foods and maintaining fitness routines to ensuring you get quality sleep, these tips form the basis for a holistic travel experience. We'll explore everything from healthcare access to preparing for unexpected situations, helping you chart a path through the myriad challenges of solo travelling.

Sustain healthy habits

This might sound banal, but having a structure gives you a sense of stability, which is much needed when everything else around you is new. So, it's important to develop a routine. Start by setting aside specific times for exercise and self-care, just like you would at home. Whether it's taking a morning walk to explore the neighbourhood or a reading session on your hotel balcony, regular activities help maintain your fitness levels and offer moments of calm.

Now, travelling opens up a world of culinary delights that are hard to resist. Yet, making nutritious food choices doesn't mean missing out on sampling local cuisines. It's all about balance. When presented with the vibrant array of a street market, opt for dishes rich in vegetables, lean proteins, and whole grains. Enjoy the flavours, but be mindful of portion sizes and preparation methods. A tossed salad or grilled fish could be as delightful as any fried delicacy. Carrying healthy snacks like nuts, fruits, or yoghurt prevents impulsive eating and keeps your energy levels stable throughout the day.

Sleep is also crucial when you're on the move. It's tempting to squeeze every ounce of daylight from your trip, but prioritising quality sleep is non-negotiable. Jet lag and varied accommodations can easily disrupt your rest. Try sticking to a consistent bedtime routine even while travelling. Small habits such as reading before bed can

© Gordon Chesterman

signal your body that it's time to wind down. Using earplugs, a sleep mask, or white noise apps creates an environment conducive to restful sleep, which is essential for keeping your immune system robust and reducing stress.

Moreover, hydration often takes a back seat amidst the hustle of travel. However, staying hydrated is vital, especially if you're exploring hot climates. For instance, Singapore is often oppressively humid in February. When I was there, I bought four bottles of water just on my first day. Fortunately, my hotel provided a chilled water fountain on my floor, so I took advantage of it. Every day before leaving, I filled the bottles and put them in my bag. Doing this not only helped me stay hydrated, but also saved a small fortune.

If you don't drink enough, dehydration may lead to fatigue, headaches, and even digestive issues, turning your dream vacation into a nightmare. So, make it a habit to carry a refillable water bottle. Many airports and public spaces now offer refill stations, so take advantage of them. To make plain water more enticing, you can infuse it with slices of lemon, cucumber, or mint. These add flavour and give you additional nutrients. Plus, avoid excessive caffeine and alcohol; both can dehydrate you further.

In addition to integrating wellness practises into your travel routine, take care of your mental well-being. Travel might be overwhelming, particularly if you're introverted, often feel anxious, and struggle to get out of your comfort zone. Incorporate practises such as mindfulness or journalling to help manage anxiety and stress. Simple breathing exercises or writing down your thoughts provides relief and keeps you centred, allowing you to enjoy the beauty and experiences of your destination without feeling overwhelmed.

Initially, developing a routine, choosing healthy nutritious foods, ensuring adequate sleep, and staying hydrated may seem hefty amidst travel spontaneity. However, these small yet powerful steps play an instrumental role in fostering your overall wellness. Consider establishing boundaries, such as scheduling breaks during city tours. As you already learned, allow yourself time to relax, whether visiting a serene park or indulging in quiet reflection.

Strategise access to healthcare services

When you are setting out on an adventure abroad, you must equip yourself with the right knowledge about accessing healthcare and preventing potential health issues. Let's explore some essential strategies that can help you stay healthy and prepared.

First things first, conducting thorough research on local hospitals and clinics at your destination is key. Knowing where reliable healthcare facilities are located can make a huge difference in case of emergencies. Before you set off, take the time to look up hospitals and clinics near your accommodation and save their contact details. This is especially important if you're venturing into areas with limited access to medical services. Keep in mind that urban areas usually offer more medical facilities than remote locations. It's wise to check the reviews and reputations of these institutions online. This way, you ensure they're reputable and equipped to handle various medical situations and know in advance if they speak your language, and you can easily communicate with them.

In fact, language barriers may well present challenges in health-related scenarios. If you can't find a clinic or hospital with staff who speaks English for example, consider carrying a phrasebook or downloading a translation app to facilitate communication in case of medical emergencies. It's also helpful to prepare a card that lists any chronic conditions, allergies, medications, and blood type in both English and the local language. These preparations enable smoother interactions with local medical staff, ensuring you receive appropriate care promptly.

An often overlooked yet critical step prior to travelling is understanding international insurance policies. Simply relying on your current health insurance may not be enough, as many standard plans do not provide coverage outside your home country. Research whether your existing plan covers international travel or consider purchasing additional travel insurance specifically for healthcare abroad. Many travellers find themselves bearing hefty out-of-pocket expenses because they were unaware their insurance didn't cover incidents abroad. Furthermore, check if your insurance includes emergency evacuation coverage, which can be vital if you need to be transported to another location for treatment. Always carry your insurance documents and the insurer's emergency contact information with you during your travels.

Vaccinations and personal medications form the backbone of your health protection against preventable illnesses. Depending on your destination, some vaccinations might be mandatory, while others are strongly recommended. Diseases such as yellow fever, typhoid, or hepatitis A might be prevalent in certain regions, and being vaccinated could save you from a serious illness. Visit a travel clinic well ahead of your departure to get advice tailored to your itinerary and health needs. Additionally, pack ample amounts of any prescribed medication you require daily. Bring these medications in original packaging along with a copy of the prescription, ensuring compliance with local regulations. Consider packing extras in case of travel delays.

Tackling these tasks might feel overwhelming, but each step increases confidence in handling your own well-being abroad. Imagine the freedom to explore your destination without the persistent worry over what might happen if you fall ill or injure yourself. Through meticulous pre-travel planning, you empower yourself to enjoy the richness and diversity that new cultures and landscapes offer without compromising your health and safety.

Prepare for potential emergencies

To handle potential emergencies, craft an emergency contact plan. Start by choosing a reliable person back home who can act as your primary contact. Ensure they're aware of your travel plans, including itinerary details and accommodations. It's also wise to provide them with copies of important documents such as your passport, insurance policy, and visa (if needed). Having your emergency contact information saved on your phone and written down somewhere accessible ensures you can get in touch even if technology fails.

Additionally, learning vervy basic first-aid skills can be helpful. Before embarking on your journey, consider enrolling in a first-aid course that covers essentials like CPR, wound care, and how to manage minor burns or sprains. These skills can help you handle common injuries effectively, providing critical care in the crucial moments before professional help arrives. Many organisations offer tailored courses for travellers, focusing on situations you might encounter while abroad, such as dealing with altitude sickness or recognising symptoms of heatstroke.

Plus, check local conditions in advance as a further layer of protection. Research your destination for potential risks, such as extreme weather events, endemic

diseases, or political instability. For instance, knowing if a region is prone to earthquakes will prompt you to familiarise yourself with earthquake safety procedures. Similarly, understanding the prevalent diseases in an area can guide you in taking preventive measures, such as vaccinations or carrying necessary medications.

Keep in mind that different countries have varied systems for handling emergencies. Some places may use specific numbers for medical emergencies, while others rely on different processes. It's crucial to familiarise yourself with how to access emergency services in your location, which could mean identifying local hospitals, clinics, or embassies where you can seek assistance. Moreover, being mindful of cultural considerations during crises—such as body language, communication styles, or local customs—affects your interactions positively and keeps you from inadvertently offending locals.

Create a concise checklist you can review before departing to ensure you're not bombarded with excessive information once there. Plus, revisit this checklist during your travels to maintain awareness and readiness and feel less anxious.

The process of planning for emergencies starts long before you board your flight. It involves thoroughly preparing for possible scenarios and making informed decisions. This preparation is crucial for travellers aiming to break free from their comfort zones. By ensuring preparedness, you reduce risks and embrace the adventure with confidence.

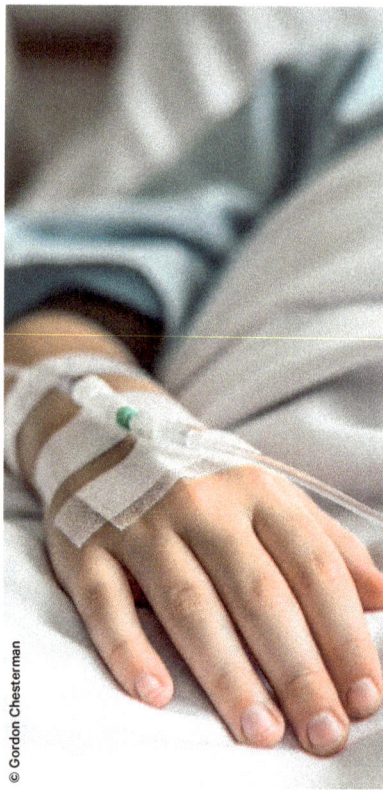
© Gordon Chesterman

Beyond the obvious benefits of emergency preparedness, this approach fosters a sense of empowerment and self-assurance. Feeling secure and knowledgeable allows you to focus on enjoying your travels, connecting with different cultures, and experiencing personal growth. With each step, from enrolling in a first-aid course to researching local emergency protocols, you invest in a safer journey.

How to deal with common travel health issues

Now, let's consider some practical tips on how to address common health challenges effectively so you can enjoy your journey without worry.

First up, let's talk about motion sickness. Nothing dampens the excitement of an adventure like feeling queasy. Fortunately, there are natural remedies and practical strategies that can reduce discomfort. Ginger is a well-known remedy; whether you choose ginger tea or candies, it works wonders in soothing your stomach. Acupressure wristbands are another great tool, applying pressure to specific points to alleviate nausea. Before travelling, identify your triggers—whether it's reading in a moving vehicle or travelling on windy roads—and plan ahead to minimise exposure. Choosing seats near the wings of a plane or toward the front of a bus also stabilises your experience and keeps nausea at bay.

Perhaps, one challenge we all struggle to talk about but that all travellers face is diarrhoea. Bacteria and parasites found in food and water might cause this unpleasant condition. To lower your risk, practise safe eating habits. Stick to bottled drinks with unbroken seals, and avoid tap water unless boiled for at least five minutes. You should wash fresh fruits and vegetables thoroughly and peel them before eating them, while you should avoid raw or undercooked meats, shellfish, and leafy greens. When dining out, opt for hot, well-cooked meals from reputable restaurants rather than street vendors. It might also be wise to pack nonprescription medications against diarrhoea as preventative measures. If you have chronic conditions, consult your healthcare provider for advice tailored to you.

Allergies may be another hurdle when travelling abroad, especially when language barriers come into play. So, communication is key to ensuring safer dining experiences. It's helpful to learn basic phrases related to your allergies in the local language or carry allergy cards that state your dietary restrictions. Translation apps or printed cards can bridge communication gaps, allowing you to express your needs to restaurant staff. Additionally, research popular dishes beforehand to choose foods less likely to trigger allergies. Always be cautious and vigilant, checking ingredient lists where possible and speaking up if anything seems unclear.

Last but not least, always check your mental health. Recognising personal triggers is the first step in managing anxiety and stress during your travels. Reflect on what typically causes unease—is it crowded places, unfamiliar settings, or lack of routine? Once identified, take proactive steps to cope. Create a flexible itinerary that includes downtime for relaxation.

Remember, preparation is your best friend when addressing potential health challenges abroad. Before you jet off, check your health insurance coverage and consider taking out travel insurance to handle unforeseen medical expenses. Pack a comprehensive first aid kit tailored to your needs, including essentials such as your prescription medications, and have a plan for accessing healthcare if needed.

Now, you are equipped with the tools to look after your health and handle any bumps in the road while you're out exploring. We've talked through some simple strategies for keeping up with healthy habits, from establishing a routine and making smart food choices to prioritising good sleep and staying hydrated. And let's not forget the importance of mental well-being—keeping a calm mind is just as crucial as maintaining physical health when everything around you is changing.

On top of that, it's vital to prepare for any number of unexpected situations. By researching the local healthcare facilities and understanding international insurance policies, you are setting up a safety net for yourself.

Here's a list of medications you may need when travelling abroad:

- Antihistamines for allergies
- Pain relievers like Ibuprofen or Acetaminophen for headaches or mild pain. If you have a chronic condition, bring medication for that, too
- Stomach medicines (antacids or anti-nausea drugs)
- Basic first aid kit that includes band-aids, antiseptic wipes, and gauze
- Medications for traveller's diarrhoea, such as antibiotics
- Insect repellent (especially helpful in tropical areas)
- Eye drops (if your eyes get dry or irritated by airborne dust)
- An epinephrine auto-injector for allergies
- Medication for altitude sickness, including motion sickness tablets

Amjd Rdwan - Unsplash

Taking steps such as learning basic first aid, carrying language tools, and being aware of local conditions boosts your confidence in handling emergencies. This preparation means you can focus on soaking up new experiences without the fear holding you back.

After all this talk about safety and health, it's time to change the subject. In your everyday life abroad, you'll have to handle money—and it's not always easy! From tips to save money to avoiding common scams, you'll learn everything about it in the next chapter. ■

CHAPTER 8

Effective money management

When we're on holiday, we're not used to caring about money. We see something—we want it, no matter if it's food or a new T-shirt. After a few days, we look at our bank accounts and realise we've spent much more than we thought. Therefore, we start feeling stressed and wonder what to do. To avoid such situations while travelling alone, you must learn to manage money effectively. It's all about ensuring you have the freedom to enjoy your solo trip without worrying about finances. Financial savvy isn't just beneficial; it's empowering, turning potential stress into smooth sailing. As you plan your journey, envision a trip where each decision reflects thoughtful financial preparation, from flights and lodging to meals and activities. A well-managed budget opens doors to spontaneous side trips or local delights that might otherwise seem out of reach.

In the next sections, you'll learn strategies to craft a realistic budget aligned with your travel goals. We'll cover everything from categorising expenses for clarity to setting spending limits that keep your wallet happy without sacrificing fun. You'll also discover how flexibility within your budget allows for unexpected surprises—both good and bad—so you're prepared for whatever comes your way.

Form a realistic budget

The first step to managing money effectively is forming a realistic budget. Budgeting properly alleviates a lot of the anxiety associated with solo travel and allows you to fully immerse yourself in the experience.

Start with breaking down your potential expenses into manageable categories: accommodation, food, transport, and activities. This categorisation helps you organise costs and provides clarity on where your money is going. For accommodation, consider options ranging from hotels to hostels or even rental apartments, as you learned in Chapter 6. Each choice comes with different cost implications and levels of comfort. If you do some research ahead of time, you can find accommodation that fits both your budget and comfort level.

Food is another area where budgets can quickly spiral out of control when travelling, especially if you plan to dine out for most meals. So, set a separate budget for food to prioritise spending. At the same time, keep track of your expenses both with credit cards and cash. Sometimes, you may be able to use credit cards wherever you go. Other times, your only chance of survival is having cash, as is the case in the Hawker Centres of Singapore. If you plan to go there, make sure to have some cash with you or you'll starve. In fact, nobody accepts cards there, only cash. I prepared for this, by going to my local supermarket back home. The exchange rate was good, and I even received some points on my store card, which was a nice little bonus. Initially, the cashier gave me high-value notes, so I kindly asked her to change them to lower denominations. I would have felt very bad giving the vendor in the Hawker stall a 50S$ note for a meal that was under 5S$!

Instead of eating every meal at a restaurant, consider shopping for snacks and breakfast items at local grocery stores, which are much cheaper. This is exactly what I did in Singapore to keep costs down. I booked a hotel without meals included because I prefer being free to choose when and what to eat. Therefore, I had to go out every time I wanted some food. Luckily, there was a 7-Eleven shop next door, so I used it to get snacks at the end of each day to have them ready for the next morning.

Transport expenses also affect your budget and may be necessary to move around a city. However, they vary widely depending on your destination. In urban areas, public transportation or walking might be more economical than taxis. Going on foot is not that bad, as it allows you to explore your destination more intimately and get a feel of the local life. In Singapore, my FitBit had to work very hard because I clocked up between 30,000 and 40,000 steps every day. On one day I managed to hit over 51k steps taking lots of photos along the way.

Before arriving in Singapore, I watched many YouTube videos about buying prepaid tickets for the MRT so I was prepared. However, I knew I would feel stressed about not knowing how much credit I had left on my card. Therefore, I went to my bank to turn my normal bank card into a Singapore debit card that could make all the transactions in Singapore Dollars. For a around £1 a day, they activated my card, and I didn't have to pay any other transaction or currency exchange fees. When I used it in the MRT, it worked great: I could scan it getting on and off hassle-free like a native.

In your budget, you should also plan activities, such as museum visits, tours, and local experiences. Sometimes, it might be helpful to look up free events or attractions and allocate funds for a few must-do activities. By assigning each category its own budget, you create a clear financial picture which aids in prioritising what matters most to you during your trip.

Once you've categorised your costs, define maximum spending limits for each category to create a framework for making informed decisions. It's crucial here to set realistic limits which reflect both the nature of your travels and your personal financial situation. These caps not only guide your spending but also enhance accountability, reducing the risk of impulsive spending leading to financial stress. For instance, if you're planning to stay within a certain budget for activities, this might mean opting for experiences which offer the greatest value or choosing one high-cost activity complemented by some low-cost or free alternatives.

However, while sticking to a budget is important, it's equally vital to mix in flexibility. Travel can

© Gordon Chesterman

bring unexpected opportunities and challenges, so having a contingency fund as part of your budget plan can relieve stress. Allowing for an adaptable budget means setting aside a portion of your funds to cover unforeseen expenses. This flexibility ensures you can enjoy your travels without being overly concerned about your finances.

In today's digital age, technology offers numerous tools that simplify budgeting. For instance, travel apps make managing your money while travelling much easier. Apps such as PocketGuard and Trabee Pocket allow you to set budgets, track expenses in real time, and receive reminders to keep your financial plans on track. These tools often come with features like currency conversion and category tracking, helping to maintain financial control effortlessly. You can also sync apps with your bank account for insights into your spending behaviour, making it simpler to adjust your budget as needed.

In addition to this, some money apps allow you to export expense reports to check your spending habits during the trip, which can be insightful for future travel planning. Many apps also offer the feature to set financial goals, which helps you stay motivated and stick to your budget.

Preparing a comprehensive and flexible budget is not just about limiting expenditures but enhancing the overall travel experience. By understanding your expenses, setting appropriate limits, allowing room for flexibility, and utilising travel apps, you can travel with confidence. The peace of mind that comes from knowing you have control over your finances is invaluable to enjoy your travels.

Adopt smart saving techniques

Now that you know how to keep track of your money, it's time to look at ways to save. If you want to save smart, research local pricing in advance. Before you even pack your bags, dive into the details of where you'll be travelling. Understanding the cost of living in your chosen destination helps you create a realistic daily budget. Singapore is a perfect example as it is well known for being very expensive. Many travellers underestimate how different prices can be from one place to another. For instance, a cup of coffee in Paris might set you back much more than the same brew in Bangkok. Websites and travel forums are great resources to gauge these costs. You'll want to account for accommodation, meals, transportation, and activities. By analysing these elements, you can accurately set your daily spending limits, which helps manage financial expectations and prevents surprise expenses from derailing your plans.

Once you have worked out a budget, one of the best strategies is to seek cultural experiences which don't break the bank. For example, opting for local eateries over tourist traps isn't just about savings—it's an enriching endeavour. These dining spots often offer authentic cuisine at a fraction of the cost, i.e., Hawker Centres. Plus, eating where the locals do opens doors to unique interactions and stories that large restaurant chains can't provide. A hidden gem in a side street might serve the best bowl of Ramen you've ever had, and without the price tag you'd find near popular attractions. Use apps that highlight restaurant reviews by local patrons rather than tourists; they can unveil culinary treasures often overshadowed by their commercial counterparts. This way, not only will your wallet thank you, but your travel experience will become richer and more memorable.

In Singapore, I decided to visit the famous Lau Pa Sat Hawker Centre. I really enjoyed the food and was surprised by the incredibly low price! However, I soon learned that it was better to eat outside than inside. You see, if you eat inside, you'll surely notice the ceiling fans which wouldn't look out of place on a Chinook helicopter. They certainly keep you cool with a lovely draft but can make a hot meal go cold very quickly. After the first time, I preferred eating outside. These are the types of fun experiences I had when I visited places where locals hang out rather than restaurant chains where you always know what will happen and the type of experience you'll have.

Another effective way to stretch your budget is to plan your travels during off-peak times. During those periods, airlines and hotels frequently drop their rates to attract visitors. This way, you also enhance

© Gordon Chesterman

the overall quality of your trip. With fewer people around, you get more personal space and a peaceful experience, whether strolling through a museum or hiking a mountain trail. It also amplifies personal safety since managing your surroundings becomes easier with fewer distractions and potential pickpocket scenarios.

Amidst these strategies, don't overlook available discounts. Whether you're a student, senior, or member of certain professional groups, there may be concessions waiting for you. In many places, museums, galleries, theatrical performances, and public transport systems offer reduced rates for eligible individuals. It's about knowing where to look and asking the right questions. For students, international identification cards can unlock discounts worldwide. Similarly, seniors often have access to special rates that make travel far more affordable. Be sure to inquire about these options before you pay full price. Countless solo travellers have found that taking advantage of such deals stretches their budgets significantly, allowing them to explore more destinations or enjoy added experiences without worrying about costs.

Safeguard finances against scams and theft

Another effective way of managing your money effectively is to become aware of common scams that tourists often fall victim to. You may think you know a scam when you see it, but it's not always as clear as you think. Plus, in the heat of the moment, you may not even notice it. You might consider someone just a kind person when, in reality, they're trying to scam you. Or you might be so busy enjoying your holiday that you don't realise you're paying much more than you should. As you can imagine, being aware of these scams in advance helps you prepare for them and can save you a lot of money and stress.

As always, research is your most powerful tool. Before embarking on your journey, research your destination to understand scam

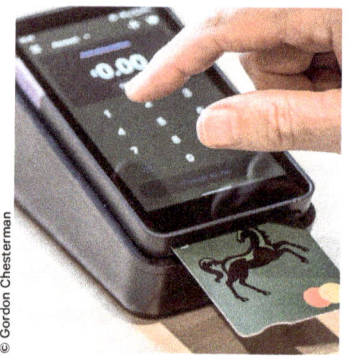

© Gordon Chesterman

hotspots and their modus operandi. This awareness arms you against deceitful tactics which prey on unsuspecting travellers. A quick look at forums or official travel advisories online gives you a good head start on what to expect. Another great source of information is again YouTube. Simply search your destination name and the word "scam," and you'll more than likely find a Youtuber highlighting the scams to be aware of. You could be surprised at the intricacies of some of them. Knowing these tactics not only boosts your confidence but also helps you navigate tricky situations skilfully, fostering resilience in unfamiliar environments.

Let's look at some common scams you may find on the street. People may offer to drive you wherever you want, pretending to be licensed taxi drivers and then charge you a lot more. Sometimes, they may be licensed and still take advantage because you're a tourist. Another typical scam happens in restaurants where you don't know the prices right from the start. You may be hungry and enticed by the amazing smells inside but when you pay the bill, you feel like being in a five-star restaurant. When choosing a place to eat, it's always better to focus on the ones that clearly display their prices, especially if you don't know the local price range. Alternatively, ask how much meals cost before sitting at a table. In touristy areas, people may also act as guide tours and charge you a lot.

In some places, bargaining is part of the everyday life. Locals might try to sell you stuff at exaggerated prices just because they know some tourists will fall for it or don't care about how much they spend. To avoid these traps, try to bargain yourself. If you feel that the price is too high for the service provided, say it's too expensive and walk away. Alternatively, pretend to have received a better offer from someone else and be tempted to

CHAPTER 8

go with them. In the beginning, bargaining might be awkward, but it's often the best way to save money.

While awareness is a must, secure banking practises add another layer of protection. Therefore, leverage two-factor authentication for all your bank accounts. This simple step makes sure that even if someone gets hold of your account details, they can't access your funds without additional proof, such as a verification code sent to your phone. Signing up for bank alerts also keeps you informed of any suspicious activity and allows you to act quickly if there's any unauthorised access. If you're using digital payment methods, check if they're secure and authenticated.

It's also wise to split your cash and cards into separate locations when travelling. Imagine misplacing your wallet or losing your bag—if everything is together, it could spell disaster. Instead, store some cash and a backup card in an alternative place, like a separate bag, money belt, or inside a hidden pocket. This way, even if one stash is compromised, you're not left helpless. It's a simple habit that makes a huge difference and provides comfort knowing you have a contingency plan.

Another factor to consider is how you use technology while travelling. As convenient as it might be to complete transactions using public Wi-Fi, it's important to resist the urge. Public networks are notorious for being insecure; hackers often exploit them to access personal information. Instead, use a private mobile network or invest in a VPN (Virtual Private Network) to encrypt your internet connection. Additionally, stick to well-known and secure payment methods when making purchases online or in stores. Many digital wallets offer excellent security features that protect your transaction data.

When planning a solo adventure, it's all about taking control of your finances to fully enjoy the journey without any worries. This chapter has walked you through forming a realistic budget which aligns with your travel goals. By breaking down expenses into categories such as accommodation, food, transport, and activities, you're better prepared to manage your spending. Additionally, adopting smart saving techniques boosts your confidence and independence during travels. Plan around local prices, choose off-peak travel, and seek out cultural activities. Plus, protecting yourself from scams and securing your finances with simple banking practises ensures a worry-free trip. These financial strategies are not just about saving money; they enhance your overall travel experience by letting you immerse yourself in your holiday.

There are many ways in which you can ensure safety abroad, thus feeling more relaxed and less stressed. For example, how you handle everyday interactions and activities plays a crucial role. In the next chapter, we'll discover strategies to become aware of your surroundings. ∎

Relax and...

© Gordon Chesterman

Be Confident but Vigilant

CHAPTER 9

Ensuring safety on the road

Once you arrive at your destination, you'll be thrilled and excited, ready to start this new adventure. You may think about the things you're used to doing at home and apply the same strategies there to stay safe on the road. However, you might not know that sometimes, you may need to apply different rules. What is effective in one country may not be in another. Ensuring safety on the road is not just about knowing where you're going but also about understanding how to keep yourself safe while getting there.

This chapter offers practical tips which will empower you to travel alone with confidence. From maintaining a sense of awareness in your surroundings to using new technology which enhances personal security, there are multiple ways to ensure that your trips are both thrilling and safe. By paying attention to these aspects, you can alleviate some of the anxieties associated with being out and about on your own. First, you'll learn to stay alert and manage your environment effectively. Next, you'll also get insights into developing habits such as making mental safety checklists and ensuring your valuables are secure.

Stay aware and adjusted to your surroundings

When you're travelling alone, being aware of your surroundings can go a long way in keeping you safe. It involves recognising key features of the environment around you. Think about it: If you're aware of potential threats and resources, you've already got a head start on reducing risks. For instance, walking down an unfamiliar street, you might notice a well-lit coffee shop or hotel where you can seek help if something feels off. These places aren't just spots for a quick break; they're potential safe havens should you need them. And it's not just about landmarks. Be mindful of exits, crowded areas, or anywhere that looks unsafe.

In Chapter 2, we looked at trusting your decisions and learning to make effective choices. These skills will come in handy once you find yourself far away from home. You must trust your intuition and gut feeling that tells you if people or situations don't feel right. Your instincts are often more reliable than you maybe give them credit for. You know that prickly feeling

when something is just off? Don't dismiss it as paranoia. Instead, look at it as a valuable tool for avoiding danger. It's like your personal radar system, keeping you safe as you navigate through new experiences. If someone's behaviour seems suspicious or a location feels dicey, there's no harm in changing your route or leaving the area altogether. Better safe than sorry, right?

Taking a step further, develop habits that keep you consistently assessing your surroundings. This means making it a routine to check your environment regularly. Are there any new faces in the area? Is that car following you? By asking yourself such questions, you stay alert and ready to react promptly. Over time, this practise becomes second nature, allowing you to enjoy your travels with peace of mind. A simple example could be looking both ways before crossing a street or periodically checking behind you in less busy areas. The idea is to maintain a heightened state of awareness without becoming overly anxious. Balance is key here; you want to be aware, but not so much that you can't relax and enjoy. A personal example of my gut feeling, was when I was shooting a timelapse on Sal Island in Cape Verde. I was on my own on a deserted beach in Murdeira Bay. I noticed a boat moving up the bay. It then turned ninety degrees making a beeline towards me. I decided there and then it didn't seem quite right. There were no tourists on board so it wasn't heading to the beach to drop people off. My immediate thought was simply, kidnap, as overreactive as that might sound. Probably totally paranoia on my part, but I didn't hang around to find out. I quickly packed the camera gear up, threw it and myself in the car and left the area.

© Gordon Chesterman

To enhance your confidence, you can also create a mental safety checklist. To do so, start by listing essential safety precautions mentally that suit your travel plans. For example, always keep emergency contacts on speed dial, know the local emergency numbers, and familiarise yourself with the basic layout of each new city you visit. Perhaps remember specific clothing items or accessories that may attract unwanted attention. Also, think about some basic phrases in the local language that can help you out if you find yourself in a sticky situation. Making these part of your regular pre-travel preparations ensures you're equipped to handle unexpected challenges effectively.

A good tip and easy habit to adopt is to walk facing oncoming traffic. If you're not used to doing it yet, it's a bit of a lifesaver because it gives you a clear view of what's ahead, helping you stay alert to potential hazards. It's also a good habit to look behind you too. Identifying safe spots along your route—such as banks or hotels—where you can stop for directions or make calls indoors rather than on the street is also wise. A good tip my father gave me, especially if you're alone and it's at night, is to walk in the middle of the road - obviously not if it's busy with traffic. If you stay on the pavement, there's a higher chance of being attacked by someone coming out of an alley giving you no time to react. Conversely, if you're in the middle of the road, you have more time to think about what to do. It makes sense really.

Another useful part of your mental checklist could be securing valuables. You should keep them in zipped compartments or front pockets. Consider using a money belt or chest pouch under your clothes to minimise theft risk, as you learned in the previous chapter. Plus, ensure your bag is on the side, away from the street, to reduce the likelihood of snatch-and-run attempts by people on foot or on scooters or mopeds.

It's also beneficial to have a plan for the accommodation you choose. Once you're there, secure your belongings and familiarise yourself with the fire exit route. Review the fire plan and do a quick walk-through to make sure you know the way. At night, have a grab bag ready to go in case of emergencies. And what about technology? Before you travel, check that all your devices are updated and avoid posting detailed travel plans on social media. During your trip, steer clear of unsecured Wi-Fi networks and keep your sensitive information under wraps. If anything feels amiss, don't hesitate to ask for a professional check once you're back.

Protect personal belongings

People who are used to travelling in groups or with their partner may consider protecting personal belongings less challenging than other problems. In fact, they always have at least another pair of eyes that can check if anyone is getting too close and trying to steal. But if you're alone, you need to rely solely on yourself to take care of your possessions.

One of the most effective ways to protect your belongings is by investing in anti-theft bags. These bags are designed with inbuilt features such as cut-resistant straps, lockable zippers, and hidden pockets, making it extremely difficult for thieves to quickly access your belongings. Brands such as Pacsafe and Peak Design offer bags reinforced with lightweight steel mesh, ensuring that even the most determined thief finds it challenging to compromise your gear.

On the other hand, RFID-blocking wallets protect against electronic pickpocketing. Nowadays, thieves can steal your credit card details without ever touching your wallet by simply scanning RFID signals emitted by the cards. An RFID-blocking wallet acts as a shield, preventing these signals from being read by unauthorised devices. This is particularly useful if you carry contactless payment cards or biometric passports. Investing in such protective gear secures your physical valuables and guards against potential identity theft.

In general, technology enhances protection in many ways. For example, GPS tracking devices and apps offer a modern solution for keeping tabs on your important items. Imagine losing your luggage or having your bag stolen while exploring a bustling marketplace—it's a nightmare scenario. However, with a device such as an Apple AirTag discreetly placed inside your luggage, you can track its location in real time using your smartphone. If misplaced, you receive immediate alerts, enabling quick actions to retrieve your belongings. The setup is straightforward: Download the app associated with your GPS tracker, define safe zones via geofencing, and enable notifications for when an item leaves this area.

Another essential strategy involves smart packing techniques. Distributing your valuables across different locations within your luggage minimises loss if a thief targets one specific bag. Utilise locked bags for items such as electronics, jewellery, or important documents. Lightweight, portable safes can secure these high-value items, deterring would-be thieves. Additionally, placing some valuables in less obvious areas, such as fabric pouches sewn into clothing linings, adds another layer of protection. This approach lessens anxiety about losing everything in one unfortunate event and contributes to peace of mind.

© Gordon Chesterman

In addition to practising these safety measures, take advantage of safe storage options in your accommodation. Many hotels offer room safes suitable for storing passports, money, and other small items. For example, my hotel safe in Singapore was fitted into a pull-out drawer which opened with a digital keypad and top lid. It was large and could easily fit my 15" laptop, lenses, power bank, and other belongings. As I care a lot about my cameras and laptop, I also contacted the hotel beforehand to verify the size of the room safe to make sure I could store them easily and securely.

Hotel safes provide a convenient and accessible option, yet it's wise to remain cautious about relying solely on them. Some travellers

CHAPTER 9

choose to use safety deposit boxes available at the hotel reception for enhanced security. These boxes typically require dual keys for access, granting an extra level of security over standard room safes.

Connect regularly with friends and family

Regular communication with loved ones plays an important role in ensuring safety while travelling alone. By maintaining consistent contact, you enhance your awareness and connection with those back home, making all the difference to both their peace of mind and sense of security.

In Chapter 3, you learned how to establish a communication plan to set specific check-in times with your family or friends. Just by doing this, you not only keep them informed of your whereabouts but also reinforce the feeling that you're never truly alone, thus reducing a bit of loneliness you may feel abroad. Suppose you intend to explore a particular city during the day; sharing your itinerary along with estimated durations and check-in times reassures everyone involved. It's like having a supportive network available at the tap of a screen, reliably ensuring that someone knows your location and expected time of return.

Smartphones today offer a host of technology features that enhance real-time connectivity. One of the most valuable tools for maintaining such connections is location-sharing apps. These applications share your live location with selected contacts, providing them with up-to-the-minute information on where you are. They also give you an added layer of security: In case of an emergency, your exact location is readily available to those who might need to assist you or alert authorities.

If you want to travel alone, you probably don't feel like having a "physical" travel buddy, but you surely can have a "digital" one. A travel buddy system involves sharing your travel plans and itineraries with a trusted friend or family member who remains your go-to contact throughout your trip. The idea isn't new—think of it similar to climbing partnerships where

© Gordon Chesterman

both climbers know each other's routes and key milestones. This means that if you miss a scheduled check-in, there is somebody who will notice and can initiate follow-up actions accordingly. This practise effectively multiplies your layers of safety, giving both you and your buddy assurances that someone is keeping an eye out for any unusual situations.

Finally, establish a comprehensive emergency response plan. It should outline clear procedures for various scenarios, such as what to do if communication is temporarily lost, how to handle medical emergencies, or whom to contact when you need urgent assistance. If you predetermine the steps to follow, you reduce panic and confusion in tense situations and ensure your support network is prepared to help you. It's also advisable to have easy access to local emergency numbers and services relevant to your travel destination, as already mentioned.

Staying in touch with loved ones is important for your well-being and peace of mind. However, remember to always balance it with independent exploration. For example, when setting regular check-ins, avoid telling your family and friends that you will text them every few hours. Instead, take some more time for yourself. You don't need to talk to them throughout the day. You can decide to dedicate a few minutes in the morning or just before going to sleep to answer messages, emails and/or make video calls. This way, you ensure that you don't keep looking at your phone while exploring, and still, you manage to keep in touch with loved ones.

Understand local customs

When travelling solo, especially to unfamiliar destinations, having a grasp of cultural knowledge significantly improves your safety and creates more meaningful and respectful interactions. While it's exciting to explore new places, understanding the local customs and traditions is key to having a positive experience.

An essential part of cultural understanding is taking time to research cultural norms before your trip. Every culture has its own set of practises, etiquette, and social rules that govern daily life. Taking the time to study these norms can be immensely beneficial. For instance, in some cultures, certain gestures or clothing choices might be considered disrespectful, while in others, they may be perfectly acceptable. Simply by familiarising yourself with these nuances, you show respect for the local way of life and avoid inadvertently offending anyone. Such an effort goes a long way in fostering goodwill with locals, as they appreciate travellers who try to understand their culture.

Another important component is learning key language phrases. Imagine finding yourself in an emergency situation—perhaps needing directions or medical assistance—and not being able to communicate effectively with those around you. Knowing even a handful of basic expressions in the local language can make a difference. Phrases like "hello," "thank you," "please," and "help" bridge communication gaps and build rapport. When locals see you making an attempt to speak their language, however minimal, it often leads to more cooperative and friendly engagements. It's a simple yet profound way to demonstrate your interest in their culture and guarantee clear communication.

To adapt to your surroundings, observe social cues and behaviours. This is not only informative but also fun! Each culture has its own set of unwritten rules about behaviour, which may differ substantially from what you're used to at home. By paying close attention to how locals interact with one another, you gain insights into what's considered appropriate or inappropriate. For example, in some countries, maintaining eye contact is seen as confident, while in others, it might be perceived as confrontational. Similarly, personal space varies globally; what feels normal to you might seem intrusive elsewhere.

By observing and mirroring these social norms, you blend in more seamlessly and reduce the risk of drawing negative attention.

Finally, engaging with locals offers a wealth of information and enriches your travel experience. One effective way to do this is by seeking out opportunities to participate in cultural events or festivals. These gatherings provide a firsthand look at traditions, music, dance, and cuisine, providing insights into the community's way of life. Additionally, participating in such activities may lead to valuable conversations with residents, who are often eager to share tips on safe areas to visit or activities to try. They might advise you on local scams to watch out for or recommend trusted service providers. But we'll look at these topics in the next chapters.

By implementing a few smart strategies and using technology, you take control of your personal safety and travel abroad with confidence. From being aware of your surroundings and trusting your intuition to creating a mental checklist and planning your accommodation thoughtfully, there are many ways to ensure that your journey stays secure and enjoyable.

Adopting these habits is like building a personal safety net—each action reinforces the others, giving you a comprehensive approach to staying safe while adventuring alone.

Modern technology is an ally in keeping your belongings intact and your loved ones informed. Whether it's using an anti-theft bag, RFID-blocking wallet, GPS trackers, or simply sharing your location with friends and family back home, technology enhances your ability to navigate unfamiliar environments securely. Remember, preparing for your trips by learning about local customs and packing wisely also plays a big role in safeguarding your experience. With these tools and techniques at your disposal, you can move beyond anxiety and embrace the thrill of travelling on your own.

Safety is important for every solo travel, but it is particularly so for women who decide to go on an adventure on their own. If you're a woman, you might look for tips to stay safe and useful techniques tailored to your needs. In the next chapter, you'll learn how to empower yourself to enjoy your travels. ■

CHAPTER 10

Tips for female travellers

Chapter 1 briefly mentioned how gender roles impact men and women differently and how society can have different expectations for the genders. However, society is constantly changing—and women, too! You probably don't want to conform to the norms but want to build independence and have your own adventures. If so, this chapter is just for you.

Thanks to it, you will master the tools you need to travel on your terms with confidence. The goal here isn't just about getting from one destination to another but creating experiences which will make each adventure totally memorable and enjoyable. You'll learn about packing the right equipment tailored to your needs and destination plus making the right choices that reflect both your style and an understanding of the diverse cultures you might encounter. You'll also discover the importance of technology in staying connected and safe and how to research destinations effectively, build meaningful connections, and use support networks while away from the comfort of your own home. Lastly, you'll learn to choose accommodation and tour operators which prioritise women's safety, creating an environment where connections with fellow travellers can flourish.

To Infinity!

© Gordon Chesterman

Last but not least, incorporate tech tools into your travel kit to boost your sense of security and ease connectivity. Personal safety alarms are handy gadgets that can emit a loud noise to deter potential threats. These small devices fit discreetly on keychains or inside pockets. Navigation apps are also indispensable, offering offline maps so you can find your way around even without internet access. Apps such as Google Maps allow you to download maps for specific areas in advance, ensuring you stay oriented no matter where you wander.

Pack specialised travel equipment

When setting off on your solo adventure, it's important to have gear that suits your needs and keeps you safe. First up is having the right luggage. For a female traveller, safety-enhanced luggage can make all the difference in ensuring your belongings are secure. Consider options with built-in locks or those made from cut-resistant materials. Many brands blend security with style, featuring compartments that are hard for thieves to access quickly, ensuring compliance with travel safety practises while still being convenient.

As you pack, remember that clothing for women travellers should be versatile and adaptable. You want pieces that are not only comfortable and easy to mix and match but also respectful of the cultural norms at your destination. A lightweight scarf, for example, can serve multiple purposes: It can cover your head and/or shoulders when visiting religious sites or double as a blanket during a chilly flight.

If you travel to hot climates, you may be tempted to bring shorts and skirts with you. Although you shouldn't eliminate those items from your list of clothes to bring, remember to have some longer pants like leggings that don't make you feel too hot but still show respect to cultures where legs should be covered. In general, you should research your destination to understand the expectations and cultural norms concerning women's clothes. Obviously, you don't need to embrace them but simply acknowledge and respect them.

Also, don't forget about hygiene and health products. Travel-sized toiletries are a lifesaver and ensure you're prepared for any situation. Think along the lines of compact sanitary products or biodegradable wipes that can easily fit into a day pack. These items are crucial for maintaining cleanliness and feeling your best on the go, particularly for flight delays or when travelling to areas where certain products may not be readily available.

Tailored safety strategies

Travelling alone for a woman is an incredibly rewarding experience which offers personal growth and a deeper understanding of the world. However, ensuring safety is a priority. Let's delve into some strategies that will help you stay safe while also making the journey enjoyable.

First, understand local laws and customs before you arrive at your destination, as already mentioned. This step is particularly important in countries where cultural practises are significantly different from what you're used to. For instance, some places may have dress codes or behaviour expectations that differ markedly from yours. Knowing these customs helps you blend in and reduces unnecessary attention.

In addition, checking for any travel advisories and understanding the safety ratings of neighbourhoods provides a clearer picture of which areas to avoid and which places are generally safe. Websites and travel advisory services regularly update their findings on crime rates and

safety measures, so make sure you consult these reliable resources. Doing this research ensures you're prepared to follow local regulations and stay on the right side of the law.

Beyond preparation, having emergency measures in place is crucial. Always carry a backup phone charger and store essential contacts both on your phone and on paper. You never know when technology might fail, and having access to numbers such as local emergency services, your country's

embassy, and trusted contacts back home is invaluable. A portable charger guarantees your phone is always powered, allowing you to communicate whenever necessary. There are carry-on suitcases with integrated charger ports which are ideal for charging all your devices in case of delays or long layovers. Plus, keep digital copies of important documents, such as your passport and visa, securely stored online.

Confidence plays an understated yet significant role in your personal safety while travelling. Walking with purpose and maintaining a visible air of confidence may discourage potential threats. Even if you are unsure of your surroundings, act confidently. Avoid looking lost, as this might make you appear vulnerable. If you need directions, stepping into a shop or café before consulting your map or phone is a good practise. This tip comes especially handy in places known for high occurrences of cell phone theft.

As well as displaying confidence, engage safely with locals to enhance your travel experience and security. While it's essential to be friendly and open to new experiences, it's equally important to trust your instincts and set boundaries when necessary. If possible, prefer talking to couples, groups of girlfriends, or simply women walking near you. This way, you reduce the chances of having a bad encounter or finding yourself in a difficult situation.

If someone makes you feel uncomfortable, make eye contact with a safe-looking person or couple close to you. In case the situation becomes dangerous, they may intervene to help you get away from it. Do not be afraid to draw attention to yourself by shouting and making a fuss, remember that being safe is more important than being polite. If you walk alone when it's dark and late, try to stay near someone who looks safe to enhance your security. As previously mentioned, walk down the middle of a street if there's no traffic. In that way, you have time to react if someone comes at you from an alleyway. Don't be embarrassed to scream at the top of your lungs to attract attention or set off a personal alarm device.

Build connections and support networks

As empowering as it is to explore the world alone, you can enrich your journey by building relationships and support networks along the way. Creating connections not only enhances your travel experience but also provides a safety net during your adventures.

To find belonging and security, you can engage in local activities and groups. Whether you join a yoga class, a cooking workshop, or a book club, these shared interests open doors to new friendships and deeper cultural understanding. By participating in these gatherings, not only do you acquire new skills or knowledge, but you also immerse yourself in the local community, fostering a sense of belonging. You become part of something larger than yourself, making your travels more meaningful and memorable.

Social media platforms have now revolutionised how travellers connect, offering vast opportunities to meet fellow adventurers virtually before meeting in person. Platforms such as Facebook and Instagram are great for joining travel groups specifically designed for women. Here, you can share experiences, ask questions, and even plan meet-ups with others who might be in the same city as you. However, it's crucial to maintain privacy and safety online. Use pseudonyms if necessary, avoid sharing detailed personal information publicly, and always meet in well-populated areas when arranging in-person encounters.

In addition, try to implement a buddy system while travelling on your own. This approach doesn't necessarily mean physically travelling with someone else but rather coordinating regular check-ins with friends or family back home, as already mentioned. Set up a schedule where you text or call every few days to update them on your whereabouts and plans. This reassures them about your safety and, at the same time, guarantees that someone knows about your locations and activities at all times. If silence persists beyond the agreed time, they can alert authorities or take necessary actions.

Also, form friendships with new acquaintances you meet during your travels for mutual support and shared experiences. Sometimes, the people you meet spontaneously become your companions for part of your journey. It might be a group from a hostel, someone from a tour, or locals eager to show you their favourite places. These interactions transform a vacation into a rich array of experiences filled with fun, learning, and lasting memories. Be open to these connections, as they often reveal the true essence of a place through its people.

Attaining the perfect balance between safety and sociability is key to having a rewarding solo travel experience. It's important to trust your instincts—if a situation or person feels off, don't hesitate to remove yourself. Always prioritise your well-being and comfort, and establish clear boundaries when interacting with new people. Remember, saying "no" when needed is a powerful tool in staying safe and enjoying your travels.

Choose women-friendly tour operators and accommodation

To ensure a safe and comfortable experience, choose the right travel services and accommodations. Dive deep into online reviews, paying close attention to comments that highlight safety features. Women-only dormitories or accommodations are increasingly available and cater specifically to female travellers. These facilities often offer additional security measures like key card access and well-monitored common areas. Women-only spaces do not just enhance safety; they create an environment where women can meet other fellow travellers, share experiences, and form connections without the fear of intrusions.

Chalermphon - AdobeStock

CHAPTER 10

If you can't find a women-only accommodation, follow some simple tips. For instance, always lock the door of your room from the inside, put something against it, like a chair, and position it so that the handle can't be pushed down if someone tries to enter. This way, you ensure nobody will disturb you in the middle of the night. Go one step further and actually take a little door wedge with you. Plus, try to avoid the ground floor, especially if there's a balcony, thus reducing the chances of intrusion. To add an extra layer of security, think about possible escape routes as soon as you arrive in your room and write them down somewhere to keep them in mind.

Selecting the right tour operator is another essential step. Do a search for "Best solo female travel operators." From the results, choose companies known for promoting safety, inclusivity, and supporting women's empowerment. Many tour operators now include women-centric tours where female guides lead small groups. These tours often ensure a respectful and insightful exploration of different cultures while making safety a priority. Additionally, ethical standards should be pivotal in your selection process. Companies devoted to sustainable tourism frequently invest in local communities, prioritising social responsibility and working toward gender equality. Consider organisations which provide assurance through guides who are not only knowledgeable about the areas but are also trained to manage emergency situations calmly and effectively.

Local insights are also invaluable. The hotel staff and local guides are excellent resources for gaining advice about which areas are safe and which situations you should avoid. They can inform you about the latest developments in local safety conditions, such as recent crime trends or notable scams targeting tourists. With their knowledge of the region, they might recommend safe transportation options and trustworthy restaurants. Do not hesitate to ask detailed questions and make use of their familiarity with the area. This information is especially helpful if you look to explore beyond typical tourist spots and dig deeper into the authentic local culture.

Plus, engage with women's travel groups. Joining these networks opens up resources and valuable insights that may not be easily available through general surveys. Plus, they provide support and confidence. Female travellers within these circles regularly exchange tips on the best places to stay, eat, and visit. Beyond practical advice, these groups inspire friendships and sharing adventures with others who value similar travelling goals.

For instance, Facebook groups, forums, and specialised travel apps dedicated to women travellers offer platforms where you can connect, share your itineraries, and even coordinate meet-ups during your holidays. This digitally connected companionship significantly eases concerns tied to travelling alone, particularly if you're introverted or naturally a little anxious.

Backup Studio - AdobeStock

Moreover, you shouldn't overlook travel insurance. This coverage acts as a financial shield against unexpected emergencies such as medical issues or cancellations, and many policies now offer specific provisions tailored for women travellers. Opting for services with a 24-7 helpline ensures you have support whenever needed and wherever you are.

Last but not least, you can also arrange airport pickups in advance to eliminate the hassle and stress of navigating unfamiliar transit systems immediately upon arrival. Most hotels and operators offer this service, providing reassurance straight off the plane. For enhanced tranquillity, verify details such as the driver's contact number and vehicle licence plate before the pickup.

As we wrap up, remember that prepping for a solo trip isn't just about filling your suitcase with essentials—it's about arming yourself with knowledge and confidence. 'Knowledge is power'. We've covered how choosing the right gear, including safety-focused luggage and versatile clothing, makes your journey smoother and safer. Don't overlook tech tools such as personal alarms or travel apps—they're like little travel buddies tucked in your pocket!

Beyond packing, we've also explored the power of preparation and connection. Researching your destination helps you respect local customs and navigate safely. It's also a huge help to have emergency contact lists ready and tech backups such as portable chargers. Engaging with locals or joining group tours enriches your experience and adds that extra layer of safety. Trust me, stepping out of your comfort zone not only boosts your confidence but also opens up a world full of amazing adventures. So, embrace these strategies and set off with the assurance that you're well-equipped for an incredible holiday on your own.

At this point, we've tackled the most effective strategies to stay safe for everyone who wants to embark on a solo journey. Now, it's time to look closer at fun solo activities that you can engage in while travelling. ∎

© Gordon Chesterman

CHAPTER 11

Cultivating hobbies to enhance your experience

Solo activities are not just a way to pass the time but tools for your personal development and also cultural immersion while on the road. Engaging in individual pastimes opens up a world of opportunities to enrich your journey, connect with new surroundings, and uncover aspects of local life you might otherwise miss. Whether you're photographing a sunrise or jotting down thoughts in a journal, these solitary pursuits offer a channel for self-expression and growth that enhances your travel.

In the next sections, we'll delve into various hobbies, focusing on their potential to boost your travel experience. From learning photography techniques that allow for capturing amazing moments to experimenting with writing that paints vivid narratives of your experiences, we'll explore how these activities enrich your trips. We'll also look at the role of exploration through hobbies like hiking, which promotes independence and mindfulness, setting the stage for personal growth.

A beginner's guide to travel photography

Photography allows you to see the world around you in new ways and capture moments that evoke emotions long after you've left the location. No matter if you're using a professional camera or a smartphone, understanding your gear impacts your creative expression.

Cameras vary widely in their capabilities, ranging from compact smartphones with impressive built-in cameras to sophisticated digital single-lens reflex cameras (DSLRs) with interchangeable lenses. Each type offers unique advantages; for instance, smartphones allow for quick candid shots while DSLRs provide greater control over settings like aperture and shutter speed.

If the reason why you take pictures is to remember the good times you had and look back on the places you visited, then smartphones have great cameras to capture your moments. In my case, I sell photos and video clips with an online imagebank. Therefore, I prefer to use professional cameras to ensure high quality.

I carry multiple cameras because I hate changing lenses—it takes too much time and can let in dust to the sensor. So, I usually have three cameras: one with a 70-200mm zoom lens, another with a 24mm-70mm, and a 7.5mm rectilinear lens for super wider shots. The last one allows me to shoot buildings and scenes without them bending in from the sides.

You can't imagine the doors a big lens can open! Thanks to it, I've seen places no normal tourist could visit. For instance, I've been allowed access to roofs of office buildings to get an aerial shot with my cameras and white lenses (and a subtle flash of my Canon CPS membership card).

If you gain entry to a building via your cameras, it's good practise to

CHAPTER 11

show respect. For example, I went to the Skai restaurant on the 70th floor of the Swissôtel, The Stamford. After obtaining permission from the concierge on the ground floor, I introduced myself to the restaurant reception and explained what I wanted to do. I then put on a single cloth glove, to their intrigue—not to look like Michael Jackson, but to help me with window shots.

I was as professional as possible and made sure to leave the huge glass windows clean.

Practical tips for newbies

If you're new to photography, start by exploring basic settings such as ISO, which adjusts the camera's sensitivity to light, and aperture, which controls the depth of field. Understanding these

shot might add drama, whereas a high-angle one provides context to your subject. Changing perspectives builds confidence and helps you interact with your environment in an engaging manner. For example, photographing a bustling market from different viewpoints might result in images that are visually appealing and also better tells a story of everyday life in that locale.

Skai Restaurant View

© Gordon Chesterman

To cut out the numerous light reflections from the restaurant, I put the lens against the glass, closed my gloved hand to seal the front of the lens against the window. In the reflection, I could see the girl watching me from behind, and I completely understood it, as her priority was their guests' privacy. I noticed that there was a restricted area, so I asked permission to take shots from there, and she agreed.

elements helps you better manage various lighting situations and bring out the best in your subjects. This knowledge empowers you to capture images confidently, knowing exactly how to adjust your camera to fit the scene unfolding before you.

Experimentation is also key to mastering photography and enhancing your travel experience. Try different angles—a low-angle

When experimenting, don't be afraid to say lie flat on the ground for ultra-low-level shots. People may look at you weirdly, but if they could see what you're seeing in the viewfinder, they'd know why. However, pay attention to people around you to avoid becoming a trip hazard. They may be looking at the sights and not notice you before it's too late. Take my word for it, I know something about this.

Composition techniques such as the rule of thirds and framing involve dividing your frame into nine equal rectangles and positioning your main subject along these lines or intersections for a balanced composition. This simple method often results in more harmonious and engaging photos. Framing, on the other hand, involves using elements within the scene, such as windows or arches, to draw attention to the subject. Such techniques create aesthetically pleasing photos and guide viewers' eyes to focus on what truly matters in the image. When done right, they elevate a picture from just a record of a moment to a piece of art which captures the essence of the experience.

© Gordon Chesterman

Photography is a very powerful narrative device which allows you to create emotional connections with places and experiences. By being intentional about what you want to say through your images, you convey the mood and atmosphere of a place. Whether it's the serene calm of a misty morning or the vibrant chaos of a busy street, each photo has the potential to transport both you and your audience back to that moment.

Consider incorporating human elements, whether it's a local vendor in a marketplace or a solitary figure against a vast landscape, to evoke emotion and offer a sense of scale. These subtle inclusions transform landscapes into relatable stories, evoking feelings of wonder and empathy among those who view your work. As a general note, ask for people's permission when you want to use them in photos to sell online through image banks. This way, you'll have no problem with copyright and issues. I take a quick video on my phone of them giving their permission, just to be on the safe side. There are also Apps which log their consent with a signature. Offering to send them a copy also works to obtain permission.

Timing and lighting are other crucial factors in capturing stunning travel photos. You probably know about the golden hours, just after sunrise and before sunset. They're named this way because they provide soft, diffused light that enhances colours and textures without harsh shadows, making these times ideal for photography. However, don't be discouraged if conditions aren't perfect. Overcast days offer even lighting without harsh contrasts, perfect for portraits and capturing subtle details. The key to taking the perfect picture is being patient and observant. This way, you may seize unexpected opportunities, turning ordinary scenes into captivating memories.

Other practical tips can improve your travel photography. For example, keeping your camera handy, regularly cleaning your lens, and making sure you have enough memory space go a long way in ensuring you're always prepared to capture that perfect shot. Familiarising yourself with photo apps can also enhance your skills. Many apps offer functionalities such as editing, filters, and sharing options, making it easier to process and showcase your work directly from your phone or camera.

GOOD TIP

Set up "presets" and save them for your most common shooting scenarios. This also applies to video presets on my Lumix GH camera. For example, my "presets" include normal daylight at 25 and 50 fps, a slow-motion setting, and one for night shoots. Having these presets cuts out 'settings stress' in the moment.

Remember that photography is a personal experience. Don't be afraid to develop your own style and let your photos reflect your emotions. Take inspiration from your travels and use your camera as a way to explore and express yourself creatively. Every photograph you take is a step toward understanding both the world around you and your own perspective on it. Therefore, don't judge yourself harshly if you don't manage to take the perfect picture—photography is much more than that.

In my case, taking photos is not just a passion but a security blanket, something that makes me feel comfortable and relaxed in new surroundings and crowded places. Without it, I probably wouldn't be able to enjoy my travels.

Ideas for journal-keeping

One way to navigate a solo travel experience is through writing, which is not only an expressive outlet but also enriches the overall travel adventure. Writing as a hobby provides an avenue for processing emotions, embracing the challenges, and deepening self-understanding during your travel. Here are some practical ways to use writing to enhance your solo adventures.

Two popular methods are free writing and bullet journalling. Free writing encourages you to express your thoughts and emotions without worrying about structure or grammar, which can be liberating and insightful. This form of writing allows spontaneous ideas and raw emotions to flow, helping you uncover feelings you might not have been consciously aware of. Think of it as letting your mind wander freely—almost like a mental detox.

Bullet journalling, on the other hand, offers a more structured approach. It combines creativity and organisation, allowing you to document your days in a concise yet personal format. Tracking daily activities, noting down places visited, and recording small achievements or unexpected finds help reflect on your personal growth to remember intricate details of your trip long after it's over, capturing moments that would otherwise fade from memory.

If you want, why not try adding drawings and doodles to make your journal more personal. Drawing what you see around you, whether it's a breathtaking landscape or a simple cup of coffee at a local café, adds a visual element to your writing. Don't worry if you're not an artist; these visuals serve as snapshots that reignite memories and evoke emotions when revisited.

Take a moment each day to write about what you saw, how you felt, and whom you interacted with to transform mundane details into meaningful narratives. As you sit down to pen your reflections, consider prompts such as:

- What was the highlight of your day?
- Did anything unexpected happen?
- How did the environment affect you?

Answering these questions fosters mindfulness and recognition of the subtler aspects of travel that can often go unnoticed.

Writing about surprises and challenges encountered during your travels also builds resilience and a sense of adventure. Travel seldom goes exactly as planned, and these hiccups are valuable learning opportunities. By documenting how you navigated these situations, you create a narrative of growth and adaptability. Whether it's missing a train or discovering a hidden gem off the beaten path, jotting down these stories encourages a mindset that welcomes unpredictability, turning potential stressors into stories of exploration.

As for example, imagine getting lost in a bustling city on the first day of your trip—a situation sure to spike anxiety levels. Instead of viewing it solely as a misfortune, use it as fodder for your journal. Describe the sights and sounds you encountered while finding your way back or any unexpected kindness from strangers which helped you feel more connected to the place. These written accounts will become reminders of your capability to overcome obstacles and adapt to new environments, reinforcing confidence in your ability to handle future challenges.

After a few trips, you may even gather enough notes, thoughts, and experiences to consider writing your own book. This is a great way to express your emotions and also help others who think about doing what you've successfully done yourself. You might even write a best-seller! Detailed journalling could pay dividends if you decide to go down that route.

If you find it difficult to start writing, consider setting aside specific times each day dedicated to it. Even just ten minutes before bed is enough. Plus, establish a routine to make it easier to integrate journalling into your travel schedule.

Hiking for independence

Imagine setting out on a trail all by yourself, with only the sound of rustling leaves and chirping birds to accompany you. This simple yet powerful activity has numerous benefits for your mental health and personal growth.

Firstly, spending time hiking in nature is like hitting a reset button for your mind. The fresh air and natural surroundings lift your mood significantly. Walking through lush greenery or along mountain paths releases endorphins, those feel-good hormones that naturally boost happiness and lower stress levels. You might find yourself more relaxed and centred after a hike, with anxiety melting away as if it never existed.

I can vouch for this personally. In Tenerife, the highest point is Teide National Park. When I lived there, I regularly went up to the observatories to shoot timelapses. At night, the skies were so clear that I could see the Milky Way with the naked eye. It was jaw-dropping! My timelapses often took around four to five hours, so I used to take a sleeping bag with me and set a timer to wake me up when the shoot was completed. With the rhythmic clicking of the shutter, I would fall asleep under the stars right away. The total quietness was deafening, the only sound being the breeze rustling the bushes now and again. These experiences on my own—with no people, traffic, or city noises—were very soothing and always helped to reset my mind and de-stress.

Keep in mind that when you embark on a solo hiking adventure, you're responsible for your safety

© Gordon Chesterman

and well-being. This aspect of hiking alone compels you to practise essential safety measures, enhancing your situational intelligence. You learn to read maps, check weather patterns, and carry necessary supplies like water, a first aid kit, and a whistle. Moreover, preparing for unexpected situations trains you to adapt quickly, improve problem-solving skills, and enhance decision-making. These skills translate well into other aspects of life, increasing your overall adaptability.

© Gordon Chesterman

As you navigate trails without a companion, you become more attuned to your surroundings and inner thoughts. Solo hikes provide a unique opportunity to engage in self-reflection and meditation, promoting mindfulness by encouraging you to live in the moment. The serenity of nature also allows you to focus on your breathing, immerse yourself in the sounds around you, and appreciate the beauty and tranquillity of the natural world. Over time, these experiences help you become more self-aware and confident in your ability to manage solitude and thrive independently.

One of the most enjoyable aspects of hiking is embracing unpredictability. Trails can surprise you with unexpected challenges or stunning vistas, encouraging a complete sense of adventure. While some paths are well-marked and predictable, others might lead you through dense forests or up rocky inclines. Such unpredictability requires flexibility and a willingness to go off the beaten path. But if you embrace these spontaneous moments, you foster an adventurous spirit, making you more open to new experiences and less fearful of the unknown.

Furthermore, hiking on your own empowers you to take control of your journey completely—choosing paths, pacing yourself, and deciding when to pause and soak in the sights. This autonomy builds confidence and instils a deep sense of satisfaction. If you're new to hiking, start simple. Choose a local trail and plan a short hike. Remember to inform someone about your plans before you head out, and always prioritise safety. As you gain more experience, you'll likely notice an increase in your physical stamina, mental clarity, and eagerness to explore further afield.

Whether traversing mountains or wandering through wooded paths, each step brings you closer to discovering your strengths and limitations. These insights pave the way for newfound independence and self-assuredness, qualities invaluable in every walk of life.

Immersive language learning

When it comes to enhancing your travel experience, learning languages in authentic settings is simply a fantastic way to boost both confidence and cultural appreciation. Engage in experiential learning with locals to really immerse yourself in the language. For example, strike up conversations with shopkeepers or join community events to practise what you've learnt. This real-world practise accelerates language learning because you're applying it in practical contexts, which improves both vocabulary and communication skills.

One of the easiest ways to learn a new language is through mobile language apps, which can even employ AI to have conversations with. These apps provide structured practise that fits neatly into any travel schedule. Options such as Duolingo or Babbel offer gamified learning experiences that keep things fun and engaging. They incorporate elements of play, thus making repetitive practise feel more like a game than a chore. It's a convenient way to keep refining your language skills daily, even while exploring new places. Plus, these apps often have short lessons that can fit in during downtime, no matter if you're on a train or waiting for a meal.

Another exciting alternative is with attending local workshops. Many places offer full cultural immersion programs where you learn the language while also engaging with local traditions. They may include cooking classes, dance lessons, or crafting workshops.

All these opportunities allow you to pick up vocabulary that's relevant to specific aspects of the culture.

If you seek to expand your language skills further, nothing beats the practical usage of language in everyday interactions. This could be as simple as ordering food in a local restaurant, asking for directions, or haggling at a market. The main key is to engage with people wherever possible. Through these interactions, you naturally strengthen your grasp of vocabulary and grammar without needing to sit down and study them traditionally. Moreover, each successful exchange boosts your confidence, encouraging more practise and interaction, forming a positive cycle of learning and reinforcing.

By focusing on the cultural aspect of language learning, you establish a purpose and context for social interactions, which can make these experiences less daunting if you're introverted or feel anxious when talking to strangers. Slowly, as your confidence grows, you'll find yourself enjoying the benefits of these engagements without feeling overwhelmed.

Beyond just visiting iconic sites or taking picturesque photos, learning the local language transforms you from a tourist into a participant in the daily life of the place you're visiting. It breaks down barriers and creates connections you might not otherwise encounter.

Moreover, the ability to converse in another language also facilitates deeper conversations with locals and provides insights into their values, beliefs, and perspectives. This level of engagement fosters a greater sense of empathy and cultural appreciation, allowing you to see the world through a different lens, so to speak. It's about building bridges and finding common ground amid diverse experiences.

Aside from the immediate travel benefits, these language skills have lifelong benefits. The ability to speak multiple languages can even enhance and open up career opportunities, opens doors to international experiences, and

© Gordon Chesterman

broadens personal horizons. But perhaps the greatest reward of all is the personal growth that accompanies stepping out of your comfort zone to embrace new challenges and experiences.

When travelling, combining your hobbies with the adventure of being alone really enriches your experiences. If you love photography, imagine capturing those spontaneous, beautiful moments that tell a story and resonate on an emotional level long after you return home. Using photography as more than a hobby allows you to connect more deeply with your surroundings, encouraging you to see places in new, inspiring ways. It's about finding creativity and joy in the process, whether you're snapping vibrant market scenes or capturing serene landscapes at dawn. Every click of the shutter is an opportunity to view the world differently and capture memories which truly reflect your unique perspective.

Similarly, integrating other hobbies like journalling or language learning transforms how you experience travel. Writing helps process feelings and challenges, turning everyday events into meaningful narratives. Hiking connects you with nature and builds mindfulness. Meanwhile, picking up a few local phrases not only eases communication but facilitates cultural interactions you might have missed otherwise.

However, travelling alone might involve much more than solo hobbies. During your trips, you may end up participating in group activities that create connections with like-minded people. ■

National Gallery Singapore

© Gordon Chesterman

Take in the History

CHAPTER 12

Connecting via group activities

James Baldwin - Unsplash

Whether you lean more toward introversion or you're bravely stepping out of a comfort zone shadowed by social anxiety, engaging in group settings while travelling helps you grow and engage in rewarding social interactions. Imagine participating in activities where you're not just an observer but a part of the narrative, building bonds over shared interests and unforgettable moments.

This chapter delves into the nuances of solo travel paired with group dynamics to enrich your experience. You'll explore how to choose the right group tours which align with your travel aspirations while ensuring safety and inclusion. You'll also learn how to find workshops to improve your cooking skills and artistic talent while connecting with others. In addition, you'll discover the power of volunteering while travelling. By the end of this chapter, you'll know the best group activities for you and where to find them.

Guidelines for selecting group tours

When planning a trip, finding the right group tour is key to balancing travelling alone with meaningful connections. In fact, it's essential to select a tour that aligns with your comfort level and travel goals. Let's look into practical advice on how you can make those choices effectively.

First off, research reputable tour companies to ensure an enjoyable experience. Companies that cater specifically to solo travellers focus on inclusion and safety, which is crucial for maintaining a sense of security. These companies often provide detailed itineraries and have experienced guides who are familiar with local cultures, enhancing your overall travel experience. For example, Exodus offers guided tours where over 50% of participants are solo travellers. This means you won't be alone among couples or larger groups (*Solo Travel Holidays, n.d.*). By choosing a company that prioritises your needs as a solo traveller, you embark on adventures confident in your safety and preparedness.

A useful tip when choosing the right tour is to consider the size of the group. Smaller groups, typically around 8–16 people, often facilitate deeper connections and more intimate interactions without feeling overwhelming. In this setting, you might bond over shared experiences and stories. Conversely, larger groups may offer diverse interactions but can sometimes lead to feelings of being lost in the crowd. Thus, identifying an optimal group size that suits your social comfort significantly elevates your travel experience.

Another crucial element involves understanding the overall dynamics within a group. Assess the target audience's age, background, and interests to determine if you'll enjoy their company. For instance, some tours may attract younger travellers seeking adventure sports, while others might focus on cultural immersion suited for older participants. Websites of many tour organisers provide forums or chat spaces where travellers can interact before the trip, giving you insights into who you'll be sharing your journey with. This preliminary interaction eases anxieties by allowing you to familiarise yourself with potential travel companions and find common ground early on.

Equally important is the setting of personal boundaries during group interactions. Group travel doesn't mean you must always be socialising; it's about striking a balance between engaging with others and taking time for yourself. Being clear about your need for solitude at times is vital for managing anxiety and maintaining comfort levels. It's perfectly acceptable to skip a planned group dinner or activity if you need a break as long as you communicate openly with the group leader and/or fellow travellers. Taking advantage of the free time offered by the itinerary

© Gordon Chesterman

allows you the freedom to explore at your own pace or indulge in self-care activities like journalling or quiet contemplation of a view.

Furthermore, a growing number of tours now emphasise inclusivity and support for women travellers. Their goal is to empower female travellers and ensure safety while creating an encouraging travel atmosphere. This approach fosters not only gender parity but also a supportive network of travellers who understand each other's concerns and priorities.

Cooking and culinary experiences

There are many group activities which you can try while living your solo adventure. If you're a foodie and like tasting new meals, cooking is certainly for you. When it comes to travelling, one of the most delightful ways to connect with a culture and its people is through food. Cooking isn't just an act of nourishment but an incredibly rewarding journey into the heart of a place. By engaging in this culinary voyage, you open doors to cultural understanding and unleash your creativity.

How can you learn to cook traditional dishes? Start by joining culinary classes that focus on traditional recipes. These classes are more than just about learning how to cook; they're gateways to authentic cultural learning. Imagine kneading dough alongside a local grandma who shares stories about her childhood as she teaches you a treasured family recipe. Such experiences have the power to improve your cooking skills and give you insights into history, traditions, and daily life. Not to mention, they create opportunities for social interaction with fellow travellers, locals, and chefs, building a sense of community and shared enthusiasm for food. You can search online for information about organised culinary classes in your destination.

If you're not into cooking or don't feel comfortable in similar situations, you can also try guided food tours. If you do some research, you'll surely find some tours organised by locals who bring you to their favourite restaurants and places to eat or show you the best ones in town. They ensure you enjoy the food you try, provide invaluable tips on the local cuisine, and reveal culinary gems that you might have never found by yourself or with TripAdvisor. They may show you how they usually eat their food and

their traditions and customs. This comes in handy, especially if you visit places where chopsticks are the only things you can use to eat, but you have no idea how to use them!

Alternatively, explore local markets, which are vibrant hubs of culture. As you navigate through stalls bustling with activity, take note of the variety of produce available. Each ingredient has a story to tell about the region's climate, agriculture, and culinary habits. Try engaging with vendors in conversation or haggle over prices to improve your language skills and develop a deeper appreciation for their local way of life. Plus, familiarising yourself with native foods may inspire new recipes and creative twists on your favourites once you're back home.

Another enriching experience is connecting with locals to learn their cherished family recipes. Sitting around a bustling kitchen, listening to tales that have been passed down through generations while preparing dishes with them, creates a profound connection which goes beyond any touristic surface encounters. You won't find these personal stories in guidebooks, and they add layers to your understanding of the culture.

You'll often discover that many families take pride in their culinary secrets and are eager to share these with an enthusiastic learner. If you become friends with some locals and show enthusiasm about their food, they're very likely to invite you to their house and try what they usually eat. In some cultures, you don't even need to spend a lot of time with them—some people will meet you once and immediately be happy to show you their house and eat together!

Through these activities, you begin to view cooking as more than just meal preparation—it's an art form. It becomes a medium for expressing creativity and storytelling, reflecting both the cuisine's roots and your personal touch. The absolute joy derived from experimenting with spices or techniques is akin to painting a canvas or writing poetry. It's about creating something that's personally meaningful and yet universally appreciated—a dish that tells a story of where it's been and where it's going.

By immersing yourself in these culinary experiences, you'll gain useful life skills and a newfound confidence. The ability to replicate a local dish back home is proof of your adaptability and willingness to step out of your comfort zone. These moments stay with you, feeding your desire for further exploration and encouraging continued growth.

Cooking can be daunting, and you may feel anxious about stepping into a foreign kitchen or questioning if they'll live up to expectations. However, remember that these endeavours are meant to be joyful and liberating. Rather than focusing on perfection, embrace the process and the connections made along the way. Mistakes become memorable stories, and every attempt is a step toward greater discovery.

Exploring artistic talents

Art is arguably the most genuine way in which you can connect with someone else and the places you visit. At the same time, it's a healthy outlet that allows you to express your thoughts and emotions freely. For example, sketching is a powerful tool for self-expression and mindfulness, especially if you use it to document travels. As you sketch scenes from your journey, you engage deeply with your immediate surroundings, capturing details which might otherwise be missed in the hustle of travel. This practise anchors you in the present moment and enhances patience and concentration.

To help elevate this experience, you can try attending local art workshops. These will provide structured environments to hone skills and explore new techniques. They are more than just a learning opportunity, they offer a platform for social interaction and cultural exchange. Engaging with fellow artists from diverse backgrounds enriches your understanding of different cultures and helps foster a sense of community. These interactions also offer fresh perspectives on art and travel, broadening your outlook and inspiring new creative expressions. Workshops often take place in local studios or scenic locations, providing unique chances to place yourself in different artistic and cultural settings.

You can find art workshops by exploring local listings, community centres, and online platforms which specialise in creative courses and events. Social media groups and travel forums often

feature great recommendations or announcements for upcoming workshops, making it easier to discover opportunities wherever you are. Many cities have art supply stores that provide bulletin boards with flyers advertising classes and workshops.

In popular tourist areas, studios often host seasonal workshops that cater to visitors. These workshops may focus on specific techniques such as watercolour, pottery, or life drawing, allowing you to choose what interests you the most.

Additionally, some organisations offer themed retreats that combine art instruction with immersive cultural experiences, including local cuisine or music. Joining such a retreat deepens your understanding of the culture while developing artistic skills. You may even create long-lasting friendships with other travellers who share your passion for creativity.

Art festivals are another excellent place to find workshops. Many festivals invite artists to conduct short classes or demos, allowing its attendees to try their hand at different mediums. These events showcase local talent and also introduce visitors to regional art forms. It can be an exciting way to step out of your comfort zone and experiment with different styles. For example, you might find a master potter leading a practical hands-on workshop in a stunning outdoor setting or a street artist teaching you mural painting techniques in a vibrant neighbourhood starting you on a road to be the next Banksy!

CHAPTER 12

If you engage in conversations with artists or teachers, you may discover ongoing workshops or private lessons which might not be publicly advertised. Often, instructors are happy to share their contact information or point you to upcoming events that align with your own interests. They also provide insights into art history and techniques unique to the area, enriching your travel experience even further.

Universities frequently offer community education programmes which include art workshops for all skill levels. These institutions might host guest artists and provide a more structured learning environment. Enrolling in a class during your travels might lead to unexpected connections and build friendships, especially if you're a student yourself.

local initiatives while exploring their artistic sides. The welcoming atmosphere of these programs enhances your experience in a new location, giving you a chance to engage deeply with the culture and with other like-minded people.

Practising live sketching

If you don't feel like attending art workshops or don't feel comfortable with them, you can practise live sketching while travelling. Whether it's capturing the bustling life of a marketplace, the quiet elegance of a historical monument, or the serene beauty of a natural landscape, live sketching demands focus and dedication. This form of art requires you to be fully present, taking note of subtle shifts in light, shadow, and movement. It's a rewarding challenge that sharpens observation skills and heightens awareness

Filled with sketches, notes, and perhaps snippets of inspiration from various places, it becomes a tangible testament to your journeys. Whenever you revisit these pages, you'll relive the emotions and discoveries of those moments. Sharing your sketchbook with others may also spark interesting conversations and shared interests, connecting you with people who resonate with your experiences. Through this sharing, you inspire others while reinforcing your own growth.

If you want to break out free from your comfort zone and the fears associated with travelling alone, the act of sketching is a structured activity that offers space for reflection while gently pushing boundaries. If you decide to participate in group settings such as workshops dedicated to

© Gordon Chesterman

In addition, many towns and cities have non-profit organisations dedicated to the arts. These groups often run accessible and affordable workshops to promote community engagement. Participating in these workshops allows you to support

of the world's complexities. By engaging in live sketching, you'll create more vivid memories as each line and shade etched onto your paper tells a story of its own.

Create a visual sketchbook to chronicle your travel experiences.

sketching, the focus remains on creativity rather than forced social interactions. This way, you can keep anxiety at bay while having some genuine conversations. Therefore, you have the time to reflect and stay by yourself while also having the opportunity to talk whenever you feel like it. Gradually, this builds confidence not only in artistic abilities but also in interacting with others.

While sketching, remember that the output doesn't have to be perfect. The essence lies in the process—the freedom to express your thoughts, capture fleeting impressions, or experiment without judgement. Art is made of mistakes and experimentation. Techniques vary, from quick doodles to detailed renderings. So, there's no right or wrong approach.

Art can also improve your mental health by helping you release stress and by introducing a playfulness that alleviates the weight of routine challenges. In fact, simply setting aside time to sketch ensures intentional pauses throughout your travel, thus offering moments to decompress and reflect and promoting emotional health and overall happiness.

Volunteering

Volunteering is a great way for you to give back to the communities you visit. When you participate in volunteer activities, you create a deeper connection with the places you explore. In turn, this connection might lead to lasting memories and a sense of fulfilment.

The first step in to making a meaningful impact is identifying genuine volunteering opportunities. Research reliable organisations that align with your values. You can easily recognise them by their solid track

© Gordon Chesterman

record and clear information in their mission statement. Learning about the organisation's goals helps you choose causes that truly resonate with you. For example, if you're passionate about environmental issues, you might seek out a local conservation group, while another person interested in education could look for programs that support local schools.

Working with these types of organisations promotes trust and respect amongst volunteers and local communities. When you clearly understand the mission of your chosen organisation, you engage with the local community more effectively. This understanding leads to personal satisfaction and deeper connections with the people you meet, making your travel experience more fullfiling.

Another aspect of volunteering is understanding the specific needs of the community. You should focus on local issues and tailor your efforts accordingly. Addressing the genuine needs of the community ensures that the time and effort you spend volunteering yield positive outcomes. For instance, if a community lacks access to clean water, you could work on projects that provide water filtration systems.

By acknowledging local needs, you show cultural sensitivity and awareness. This approach develops trust and goodwill between you and the local residents. Over time, successful volunteer projects can promote long-term benefits for the community. If you and other volunteers consistently collaborate with locals, you create a lasting impact, even after your short-term stay. This teamwork often leads to improvements in community resources, education, and economic development. Therefore, don't feel awkward when applying for volunteer work in an organisation—you have the power to make a difference, because each individual's help counts.

In addition, you can also take advantage of your volunteering activities to engage with locals. This way, you open up pathways for cultural exchange and authentic experiences. Building relationships with community members leads to insights into their lives and challenges. These interactions enrich your understanding of different cultures and lifestyles. For example, sharing a meal with

CHAPTER 12

local families provides a firsthand glimpse into their traditions and daily routines.

Meaningful relationships with locals also lead to mentorship opportunities, where you gain valuable insights into overcoming local challenges. Connections create a sense of belonging which goes beyond typical tourist experiences. You may even find yourself invited to join in with community events, thus experiencing local culture much more deeply.

When you actively engage with locals, you collaborate on projects that address the community's needs. This collaboration creates shared successes, where both you and the locals learn from each other. At the same time, the friendships formed during these interactions can last well beyond the travel experience.

By volunteering, you'll discover that you can achieve genuine cultural immersion and personal fulfilment while positively affecting local communities. Engaging deeply with volunteer opportunities allows you to make lasting connections and significant impacts. As you contribute your time and effort, you also gain new perspectives on the world and your own capabilities.

Diving into group experiences while travelling alone isn't as bad as it may seem. Conversely, it's an enriching adventure that nurtures personal growth and social connections. You must pick the right group tours to balance alone time with engaging interactions, thus easing any anxiety or concern you might feel. By doing your research and choosing reputable tour companies focused on solo travellers, you ensure your travels are both enjoyable and secure.

Among the group activities you can try, the most rewarding ones are certainly cooking, art workshops, and volunteering. By participating in cooking classes and knowing more about local food, you learn ancient traditions and new dishes you can bring back home with you. Art workshops allow you to express yourself and find the perfect balance between social interactions and time by yourself. Finally, volunteering encourages you to make a concrete change and improve the local environment, thus connecting to your destination on a deeper level.

All these activities are enriching in many ways, but you may still have doubts about diving into them, especially if you don't feel comfortable around people. That's why the next chapter will be completely dedicated to useful tips and strategies to improve your communication skills and build meaningful connections. ◾

CHAPTER 13

Tips for meaningful social interactions

Do you struggle to interact with strangers in your home country? You may think it would be impossible for you to do it in a completely new place. However, you can't imagine the power travel has over our beliefs and thoughts. While travelling, you'll probably be forced to talk to others for one reason or another, especially if you travel alone. If you go unprepared, you might feel overwhelmed and anxious. But if you follow some simple tips and put effective strategies into practise, you equip yourself with the tools to handle conversations with confidence.

First, you'll learn about the art of connecting with others while maintaining personal balance. You'll discover techniques for fostering genuine interactions without feeling anxious. Then, you'll delve into how acts of kindness bridge cultural barriers and ways to befriend and integrate with locals. In other words, this chapter is packed with insights to help you make the most out of social encounters on the road.

Building authentic relationships on the road

Embracing your vulnerability, plus immersing yourself in local experiences, using technology wisely, and practising kindness, you can forge meaningful relationships with people from all different backgrounds.

To begin with, vulnerability is not always seen as a strength, but it's incredibly powerful when forming new connections. Opening up about your own experiences or challenges invites others to share theirs, creating a space for mutual understanding and empathy. For instance, sharing a personal travel story with someone might prompt them to open up about their cultural background or personal life. This exchange builds trust and lays the groundwork for deeper relationships. Don't be afraid to take that first step in being vulnerable; it can pave the way for a rewarding interaction. Remember, showing vulnerability doesn't mean oversharing every detail of your life but rather being authentic and honest in your interactions. Think of it as creating an opportunity to connect on a human level beyond the superficial conversations often encountered on the road.

In particular, feel free to talk about your vulnerabilities, such as negative feelings, fears, and anxieties. You may believe you're the only one facing these challenges and close yourself off. However, there are many people out there—like me, for instance—who struggle just as you do. If you're open to sharing your personal experiences, you may create deep connections, and maybe you'll discover a few tips about overcoming your concerns.

To establish authentic social connections, you can also engage in local experiences. Participating in festivals, workshops, or even simply enjoying a meal at a local eatery provides a window into the culture you're surrounded by. These activities not only help you understand local traditions better but also create shared experiences with the locals and fellow travellers. As mentioned, attending a local pottery class or joining a cooking workshop, are examples of activities that allow for shared learning and collaboration, which may lead to genuine friendships. Through these interactions, you will likely meet individuals who share similar interests, making it easier to strike up conversations and build relationships.

Moreover, leverage technology thoughtfully to facilitate initial conversations, especially if you find face-to-face interactions a little daunting. There are many apps and social media platforms designed to connect like-minded travellers and locals. Apps such as Meetup connect you with groups in various cities that cater to specific interests, whether it's hiking, photography, or book clubs.

Online forums and travel-focused social media communities are also excellent platforms for connecting with others before arriving at your destination, giving you the chance to plan meet-ups or join group activities upon arrival. However, while technology may be a helpful bridge, it's important to transition from online interactions to real-life encounters to deepen these connections. At the same time,

© Gordon Chesterman

make sure not to overshare or give too much confidence to people you meet online. If you ever see them in person, choose public places for your encounters and avoid being alone with them.

Lastly, kindness is a universal language that cuts through cultural barriers. Simple acts such as a smile, offering help, or showing genuine interest in someone's story go a long way in building rapport. When you enter a new environment with a warm and friendly demeanour, you're more likely to receive the same in return. Engage with locals by asking open-ended questions about their culture, history, or favourite local spots. Even if you don't speak the same language fluently, gestures of kindness such as helping carry groceries or learning basic phrases in the local language demonstrate respect and eagerness to connect.

Tips for balancing socialising and solitude

Knowing people is fun, but it can also drain you, especially if you feel a bit anxious or are introverted. Therefore, it's important to find the perfect balance between solitude and interactions. Balancing social engagement with your personal time is about finding that sweet spot between enjoying those meaningful interactions and ensuring enough time for personal reflection. As you're stepping away from your comfort zone, understanding your limits becomes essential to maintaining enjoyable interactions.

First, you must be aware of your personal boundaries. Engaging socially doesn't have to mean overextending yourself or becoming drained. It's about recognising what types of social interactions energise you and which ones leave you feeling exhausted. By identifying these boundaries, you manage your energy levels more effectively and enjoy the connections you make. Likewise, it's important to listen to your body and mind. If you're feeling overwhelmed, it might be time to step back and take a break.

Imagine sitting close to someone while eating at a restaurant or food stall, and they start talking to you. In the beginning, you may enjoy this spontaneous conversation and feel

comfortable interacting with them. After some time, you feel tired of listening to them and want to go away from that situation. If you haven't finished your meal, you can get up and ask the staff if you can take it away. Next, gently tell the person that you have something important to do, such as a planned visit to a museum or simply need to go back to your hotel. You don't need to provide many details; just be clear and simple. Finally, leave and find a better spot to finish your meal. Keep in mind that your time is valuable, and you have no obligation to fulfil with that person, so feel free to go away when you don't feel comfortable anymore.

As already mentioned, scheduling solo time is just as important as planning social activities. Solo time encourages reflection and helps you process experiences, thoughts, and emotions. It's during these quiet moments that you can recharge and mentally prepare for future adventures. Whether it's taking a leisurely stroll through a new city, sitting on a bench in a peaceful park, or simply enjoying a quiet meal alone, carving out this time allows for deeper self-discovery and appreciation of the journey.

Mindfulness plays a pivotal role in enhancing both social and solitary experiences. Being present and attentive in the moment improves your interactions and creates more meaningful connections. If you practise mindfulness, you learn to stay grounded and reduce stress and anxiety associated with social situations. Thanks to it, you develop an open and accepting attitude toward the people you meet and the experiences you encounter. When you apply it during solo moments, you feel more at peace with yourself and become more self-aware.

CHAPTER 13

Being mindful truly transforms how you perceive and adapt to new environments. Techniques such as deep breathing, meditation, or simply focusing on the present moment calm your nerves and improve interactions. By practising mindfulness, you can shift your focus from worrying about past encounters or future interactions to embracing what's happening right now. In Chapter 2, you learned about mindfulness techniques to confront your fears. You can use them to enhance your conversations, too.

How to befriend locals and fellow travellers

If you travel on your own, you might want to befriend fellow travellers or locals you meet on the road. On the one hand, you may feel scared about interacting with others. On the other hand, you might be eager to learn more about the culture you're exploring and learn about other travellers' experiences and tips. So, let's explore some strategies to forge friendships with both locals and fellow travellers.

First up: Engage locally. Stepping into local scenes is a powerful way to connect with residents. Attend community events, festivals, or even neighbourhood gatherings. This allows you to immerse yourself in the local culture and customs. A warm smile and genuine curiosity will open doors to conversations. Practising open body language, like uncrossed arms and maintaining eye contact, signals approachability. It's surprising how these simple gestures can promote interaction with people who might share their stories and insights, enriching your travel experience.

CHAPTER 13

Next, find fellow travellers. It might seem daunting, but it gets easier by zeroing in on common interests. Whether through shared hobbies, such as hiking groups, photography clubs, or casual conversations at hostels, identifying mutual interests sets the foundation for companionship.

That's what happened to me during the Singapore Airshow. I purposely organised my trip during those days to take in the show. My plan for the day was to get there

© Gordon Chesterman

early and visit all the indoor and outdoor exhibits to take photos and videos and create imagery to upload to my image bank account. Going indoors wasn't only exciting but also essential, as it was very hot and stifling outside, and I needed to enjoy the air-conditioning every now and then.

While I was filming a video clip, I noticed a man in my peripheral vision who was filming a tracking shot in the same direction I was walking. When I finished the shot, the man asked me how I rated my DJI Pocket 3. We exchanged polite chit chat then, he kindly asked me if he could join me for company because he was on his own. I accepted, and suddenly, we started talking about planes and exchanging funny stories about our passion and experiences in aviation. We kept talking for three hours!

When the conversation came to a natural end, we simply parted ways, and I continued gathering the images I had in my head. I really enjoyed chatting with him, but I had my own agenda and couldn't spend all day with him. However, I still remember this unexpected situation because I'm surprised about how easy it can be to strike up a conversation with a simple question. Even if you're not the "chatty" type, you may find someone interested in talking with you while you travel. Seize the moment to improve your communication skills and maybe make a new friend.

If you need a head start, sites such as Facebook groups designed for travellers allow you to plan meet-ups with those nearby who share your passion, creating a built-in starter topic for conversation. If you don't know how to start an interaction, consider talking about your travels. Shared destinations and travel tips can deepen these conversations into lasting friendships.

In particular, shared experiences create strong bonds. Engaging in group activities such as sightseeing tours or cooking classes provides a natural setting to connect over mutual interests, as you've already learnt. These shared adventures act as icebreakers, giving you something concrete to discuss together. For example, joining a group tour not only helps break the ice but also creates opportunities to discover hidden gems of a city while bonding with others. Activities like these make it easy to connect on more than just a superficial level, as they provide real-life moments to share and revisit.

Remember, there's a fine line between being culturally sensitive and staying true to yourself. Respecting cultural boundaries is crucial, but it doesn't mean losing your individuality. Show respect for local customs and traditions by observing, listening and learning before jumping in. Awareness of cultural differences enriches your interactions and shows locals that you take an interest in their way of life. Allow room for openness and adaptability to foster a healthier exchange of perspectives. For instance, learning basic phrases in the local language, such as greetings or simple everyday expressions, not only conveys respect but also often results in people being more willing to engage.

In my case, I had no language problem in Singapore because English is the first language taught in schools, so it's used to teach all

the subjects and everyone speaks it. The other official languages are Mandarin, Malay, and Tamil.

If you don't feel comfortable engaging in some activities locals are used to doing, don't feel forced to join in. After all, preferences and levels of comfort change from one person to another, and it's okay not to like something. For example, you might discover that locals enjoy eating a certain type of meat (or insects!), but you don't feel comfortable trying it. Feel free to gently refuse to stay true to yourself and uphold your boundaries. The same is true for all scenarios in which locals feel at ease while you don't. It's normal not to be able to fully immerse yourself in a culture, especially if it's very different from yours.

Integrating with local communities

Engaging with local communities and cultures is an exciting part of solo travel that greatly fullfils your experience. When you travel this way, you create opportunities for real connections, learn about different ways of life, and gather memories that will last a lifetime.

Redd Francisco - Unsplash

If you struggle with social interactions, whether due to being introvert or anxiety, there are effective strategies to help you open up and interact meaningfully with those around you.

STAY IN LOCAL ACCOMMODATION

Choosing where you stay can set the tone for your trip. Opting for local accommodations such as hostels, guesthouses, or homestays provides a warm and inviting atmosphere. These settings often bring together locals and travellers and foster an environment of community. For instance, in a cosy guesthouse, you might find yourself sharing breakfast with a local family or fellow travellers. This might lead to spontaneous conversations about the area, food, and customs. Plus, the great advantage of these places is that they're usually cheaper than hotels and more touristy accommodations. Therefore, staying there not only saves money but also opens the door for genuine interactions.

EXPLORE OFF-THE-BEATEN-PATH LOCATIONS

To truly engage with a community, venture into neighbourhoods that tourists usually overlook. These local spots often have rich stories to tell and activities rooted in the culture. For example, instead of heading to the well-known market, search for a smaller local market where farmers sell their produce. Here, you can chat with locals about their products and perhaps even learn how to cook a traditional dish using the ingredients you buy. Discovering these hidden gems makes your travel experience more authentic and personal.

BE OPEN AND APPROACHABLE

Approachability is key to making connections with locals. A genuine smile and a friendly demeanour go a long way. When you visit cafés, shops, or parks, don't hesitate to strike up conversations. You might ask for recommendations on what to do or simply share a little about yourself. This openness may lead to interesting discussions about daily life, customs, and even friendships. A simple greeting in the local language also breaks the ice and shows that you value their culture.

ASK FOR RECOMMENDATIONS

Locals are often proud of their town and happy to share recommendations. When exploring, take a moment to ask for advice on places to eat, things to do, or sites to see. Most locals appreciate being asked for their insights, and this helps create a dialogue where you can learn about the culture while they gain from the interaction. For instance, asking a shopkeeper about their favourite restaurant might lead you to a cosy spot that's not in any guidebook, where you can enjoy authentic local food.

JOIN A LOCAL TOUR

Another great way to learn deeply about a new place is to participate in tours led by people from that area. Local guides provide unique insights and stories that you won't find in a standard travel brochure. They offer a perspective on the culture, history, and hidden highlights that only a local might know about. Look for walking or biking tours in smaller groups; these settings often allow for more questions and connections, thus giving you a deeper understanding of the community.

VISIT COMMUNITY CENTRES

Spending time at local community centres provides a window into the life of the area. Everywhere around the world, places such as libraries, community centres, or parks are gathering spots for residents. Moreover, engage with programs or events there to get in touch with local traditions and activities. For instance, attending a free class or community event may introduce you to locals and create shared experiences. At the same time, the relaxed environment helps ease any initial anxiety about meeting new people.

USE PUBLIC TRANSPORTATION

You might be tempted to travel by taxi all the time because it's easier to understand, especially if you can use specific apps for it. However, travelling on public transportation, such as buses or trains, opens up avenues for spontaneous interactions. These modes of transport are often filled with locals commuting to work, school, or social gatherings. You might find yourself sitting next to someone who is eager to chat. Don't be afraid to strike up a conversation about their city or ask where they recommend going. Such interactions provide authentic experiences that you would miss otherwise.

Integrating some or all of these strategies into your travels, you'll find that engaging with local communities becomes a rewarding part of your journey, rich in experiences and insights. Each interaction has the potential to teach you something new, making your trip not just a journey in distance but a journey in understanding.

Travelling on your own offers a unique opportunity to build genuine connections with others, transcending cultural differences and personal inhibitions. Embracing your vulnerabilities and sharing authentic parts of yourself, you invite deeper relationships rooted in empathy and trust.

Keep in mind that you should balance social interaction with time for solitude to enjoy solo adventures while staying true to your needs. Getting to know your boundaries ensures that you enjoy energising interactions without the feeling of being overwhelmed. Finally, follow some simple tips to ensure you integrate with local communities easily, such as riding on public transport or joining local tours.

At this point, you have all the tools you need to enjoy your solo travel and reduce your concerns and anxieties. You know how to effectively interact with locals and befriend fellow travellers while staying safe and dedicating some time to yourself. However, the journey doesn't just end at your destination—it continues throughout your life. Once you come back home, you'll share your experience with others and bring back useful insights about the world and yourself. ■

CHAPTER 14

Returning home and reflecting on your journey

When you return home after an amazing solo holiday experience, the first thing you probably do is unpack your bags and check all the souvenirs you brought back with you. However, you bring back more than just some cool objects and nice pictures—you also have all the new skills you acquired on the road. The magic of travel doesn't have to fade once you settle back into your usual routine; instead, it can spark a transformation in how you view and interact with your everyday environment. This chapter helps you reflect on your journey and explores ways to seamlessly incorporate those extraordinary experiences into the fabric of daily life, ensuring that the personal growth and fresh perspectives gained abroad continue to enrich your world at home as a new you.

As you read this chapter, you'll discover strategies to integrate into your typical day-to-day routine activities. You'll also learn how viewing your local surroundings with a traveller's eye can reignite a sense of discovery and inspire personal growth. From engaging with your community in new ways to introducing spontaneity into your schedule, this chapter offers a guide to maintaining that adventurous spirit long after your return flight lands. Get ready to see how your journey continues to unfold at home!

Bringing travel experiences into your daily life

Returning home inspires a fresh perspective on everyday living. To effectively incorporate the positive experiences from your travels into your daily life, you can apply some simple strategies.

One of them involves exploring your local community as if it were a new travel destination. Consider taking a different route during your morning walk or run. You might discover hidden gems, such as small parks or unique cafés that have been right under your nose all along. This simple change brings the thrill of discovery that you experienced while travelling. The idea here is to look at your surroundings with a traveller's curiosity, even if they're places you see every day.

Plus, engage in local events to inject a sense of spontaneity into your life akin to the excitement found in travel adventures. Attend local farmers' markets, art shows, or community festivals that you might typically overlook. This not only supports your community but also allows you to experience different facets of it, similar to

how engaging with local cultures made your travels enriching. These activities encourage stepping out of your comfort zone and foster social connections, which are vital for your growth.

Spontaneity doesn't stop at just attending events; it involves being open to unexpected opportunities. If a friend invites you to try a new restaurant or attend a last-minute event, seize the chance not the safety of the sofa. Much like those not only breaks monotony but also brings back the relaxation and happiness you experienced in your vacations.

Another approach is transforming banal chores into fun explorations. Grocery shopping doesn't have to be a repetitive task; visit different markets around town instead of sticking to the usual one. This might expose you to a variety of foods, much like exploring food markets in foreign lands. Plus, trying new travel into your lifestyle. Keeping a journal or blog about your local adventures serves as a creative outlet and a means to relive those moments, as you already learned.

Last but not least, incorporate mindfulness in these activities. For instance, practise gratitude for simple pleasures, such as the beauty of a sunset or the taste of a homemade meal, to keep the essence of travel alive. Travel often teaches us to appreciate the

© Gordon Chesterman

impromptu decisions on the road that led to memorable experiences, allowing room for spontaneity in your daily life may lead to new adventures and connections.

One habit for bringing travel vibes into your life is organising travel-inspired outings. If you enjoyed hikes or picnics during your travels, incorporate these activities into regular weekends. Picnics, for instance, offer a lovely escape from routine. Choose a park, pack some food—perhaps inspired by a cuisine you loved abroad—and enjoy a day outside. This practise recipes inspired by your travels is another enjoyable way to relive those experiences at home.

If you like planning your trips, create mini-itineraries for local excursions. Design a day schedule that mimics your travel days—perhaps starting with a spot to have breakfast, followed by a visit to a bookshop or museum you've never been to, and ending at a cosy cafe. This not only helps maintain the excitement of travel planning but ensures weekend boredom is kept at bay. Moreover, document these experiences to further integrate little things, and continuing this mindset enriches our daily lives. If you already started practising mindfulness before leaving for your solo travel, it won't be hard to keep doing it once you return.

Remember, integrating travel into your routine isn't about replicating past journeys exactly, but rather capturing their true essence—the sense of wonder, adaptability, and openness they created. By doing so, you'll not only enrich your own life but influence those around you to embrace a more adventurous and fulfilling daily existence. Travel has the power to expand your mind. Even if physically far from exotic places, adopting this traveller's mindset unlocks a new passion for life right at home. Embrace these practises to sustain the feelings of the sheer satisfaction associated with travel, thus improving your mental well-being in the long term.

Enhancing relationships post-travel

You might not be aware of it, but travelling on your own provides a unique toolkit of skills that are highly transferable to your everyday life, particularly in your professional and personal relationships. Let's delve into how these experiences foster improved communication, build emotional resilience, and enhance cultural awareness.

First of all, travelling alone invites you to engage with diverse cultures and individuals, often requiring you to navigate language barriers and different social norms. This exposure naturally sharpens your communication skills. Storytelling becomes a vital tool; it's not just about swapping tales but also connecting with others on a deeper level. Crafting your narrative in a way that captivates and communicates clear messages is an art in itself that may translate directly to your workplace and social circles.

For example, If you master the ability to succinctly convey ideas, you enhance your presentations at work. You can also express your thoughts and feelings more effectively in personal relationships. When telling a story from your travels, focus on creating vivid imagery and emotion, which draw listeners in and make your message memorable. You can apply this method to professional settings, too, where conveying complex information clearly is crucial. Therefore, practising storytelling might become a way to improve your verbal communication skills and make interactions more impactful.

In addition to that, solo travel inherently involves navigating challenges—missing a train, dealing with unexpected weather changes, or managing logistical mishaps. Each of these situations requires quick thinking and adaptability, thus fostering emotional resilience, which is also invaluable when facing work-related pressures or personal life challenges.

Handling difficult circumstances during your holidays teaches you to stay calm under pressure, an essential skill in high-stress work environments. For example, if you've successfully navigated a foreign city without speaking the language, you're likely to approach workplace obstacles with a sense of confidence and composure. Moreover, this new resilience helps you manage conflicts in personal relationships by approaching disagreements with patience and understanding rather than emotional reactivity.

To help cultivate this resilience, reflect on past travel challenges and how you overcame them. Use these reflections as mental exercises to prepare for future stressors. Recognise the growth you experienced through these challenges and let it reinforce your belief in your capabilities.

Travel also exposes you to various cultural practises and perspectives, broadening your understanding and appreciation of diversity. This heightened cultural awareness significantly benefits your interactions in multicultural workspaces and social settings, as it allows for more inclusive and harmonious environments.

If you're more culturally aware, you will recognise and respect differences in attitudes, values, and communication styles. At work, this understanding produces more effective collaboration within diverse teams, where acknowledging cultural nuances prevents misunderstandings and fosters a more cohesive working environment. On a personal level, it allows you to connect with people from different backgrounds, thus enriching your life with varied experiences and viewpoints.

A great way to enhance your cultural awareness is by remaining open-minded and curious about the world around you. Try to learn from each interaction, whether it's understanding different business etiquettes or embracing unfamiliar traditions. These experiences will enrich your perspective, making you more flexible and inclusive in your relationships.

Applying travel-gained skills

In addition to the above skills, you can learn many more while travelling alone. As you return from your trips, consider the immense power these experiences have given you.

One of the most significant takeaways from solo travel is the enhanced ability to solve problems and adapt. When you're on your own in unfamiliar environments, you quickly learn to think on your feet. Perhaps you missed a flight connection or found yourself without a place to stay for the night. These situations force you to come up with creative solutions and adapt swiftly to changing circumstances. This newfound adaptability isn't just for navigating foreign cities; it's a tool that makes everyday challenges more manageable back home. For instance, when a project at work suddenly shifts direction, you can rely on your ability to adapt on the fly. To nurture this skill, set small challenges for yourself regularly—whether it's taking a different route to work or finding a new solution to a common household task. By doing this, you maintain your flexibility and creativity.

Solo travel also improves your confidence in decision-making. Managing a travel itinerary alone means making countless decisions daily—from what to eat to which sights to see—and owning those choices. It's empowering to realise that you're capable of planning and executing an entire trip independently. You can carry this trust in your decision-making abilities over into everyday life, from choosing a new career path or simply picking a restaurant for a group dinner. In all situations, you'll likely find yourself more assured in making choices.

Moreover, time management skills acquired from travelling lead to better scheduling efficiency at home. Consider the hours spent meticulously planning your journey dates, money, accommodations, and activities, all while ensuring enough room for spontaneous adventures.

© Gordon Chesterman

This skill translates seamlessly into organising your life back home, helping you allocate time wisely between work, leisure, and personal pursuits. To enhance this skill, continue practising structured planning techniques, perhaps by using planners or digital apps to keep track of appointments and deadlines, ensuring you strike that perfect balance in daily routines.

When we travel alone, we might also connect with people we meet along the way out of necessity and curiosity. This develops social skills and networking capabilities, giving even the shyest among us the opportunity to become better at initiating conversations and forming connections. You might remember the chats you had with fellow travellers or locals, breaking cultural barriers and fostering mutual understanding. Back home, these refined social skills translate into improved interactions at work and in personal relationships. Continued exposure to diverse groups, even in your locality, strengthens these skills further. Attend local events or meetings within areas of personal interest to foster new relationships and expand your network effectively.

As you reflect on your new travel experiences, cherish these newly honed skills and find creative ways to apply them. Incorporate times of spontaneity and adventure into your regular routine to keep the travel spirit alive. Recognise each challenge as an opportunity for growth and a chance to use the skills you've developed on holiday. Remember that the world of possibilities is vast—and largely untapped by our usual methods. With the tools discovered from travelling by yourself, no task is impossible. Remember, variety is the spice of life as they say.

Sharing travel experiences to inspire others

After returning home, the stories you share may well ignite the wanderlust in others, motivating them to tale a leap of faith and embark on their own journeys. It's not just about recounting sights and sounds but crafting narratives that resonate with diverse audiences. Sharing these experiences is both impactful and rewarding, especially if you're introverted or feel held back by anxiety.

CHAPTER 14

When it comes to crafting relatable stories, always keep your audience in mind. You want your tales to resonate with people who might need encouragement to step out of their comfort zones. Reflect on the emotions you felt during key moments of your travels—like fear, awe, discovery, and humour. These feelings are universal, even if the experiences aren't. By tapping into them, your stories not only become yours but also something others can see themselves in. Think about how travel taught you lessons about resilience or self-discovery.

Writing your experiences online through social media with blogs and vlogs is an excellent way to reach out to a broader audience. Platforms such as Instagram and Facebook allow you to share your journey in real time, making followers feel like they're travelling with you. If you kept a blog during your trip, continue updating it even after you return. Blogging provides a space where you can delve deeper into your experiences, offering insights that might help others prepare for similar trips. Guest posting on other travel blogs also expands your reach and gets your stories in front of new eyes. You may not believe it, but a well-crafted post could go viral, motivating potential travellers who stumble upon it unexpectedly.

Personally, I don't blog or vlog on my trips, I'm too busy taking photos However, if you do like blogging, make sure your online name can't be traced back to your home address and residence. This way, you protect your identity and can write about your travels without worrying about your house being a target for opportunist thieves.

In addition to telling your stories online, you can organise local events or workshops to share your travel knowledge and inspire others directly. For example, hosting a travel-themed night at a local café or community centre might draw in fellow adventurers eager to hear firsthand accounts and tips. Consider structuring these events around specific themes—such as budget travel, solo navigation, or cultural immersion—to cater to varied interests. On the other hand, workshops provide a more hands-on approach, where participants engage in activities that might include mapping out itineraries or learning basic phrases in a foreign language, all while soaking up your personal stories.

These gatherings inspire and foster networks among people with shared aspirations. Attendees might find travel partners or mentors among the crowd, creating a supportive community eager to help each other achieve their travel dreams. If you've managed to overcome social anxiety through travel, sharing this transformation gives hope to others struggling with

© Gordon Chesterman

similar issues. Your story becomes a testament to what's possible, a beacon guiding others toward their own path of growth and exploration.

Remember, while storytelling is powerful, authenticity is key. Be honest about your experiences, including the highs and lows. Not every day of travel is perfect, and acknowledging difficult moments makes your narrative richer and more trustworthy. This honesty builds credibility and shows prospective travellers the multifaceted nature of exploring new places. It reassures them that they, too, can handle whatever obstacles arise.

To amplify the impact of your stories, consider becoming a mentor. Reach out to universities or travel organisations to speak about your experiences. Programs seeking peer mentors for students planning to study abroad often welcome alumni travellers who can offer practical advice and inspiration. Alternatively, try going to a local school to talk about your travel adventures and how technology helped you. This might be particularly interesting for students taking tech-based courses, for example. Similarly, volunteer with nonprofits engaged in global missions or environmental projects and share your insights at their events. Such engagements stretch your influence, allowing your stories to inspire diverse groups.

As you share your narratives, keep in mind that the process isn't just about giving—it's a loop of growth. Articulating your experiences helps you reflect and integrate the lessons learned during travel into daily life. You might discover new interpretations of those experiences long after the journey ends. This cycle of sharing and reflecting makes sure that your travels continue to enrich your life and the lives of others.

In this chapter, we have explored how the skills and experiences gained from travelling alone can really light up your daily routines. By embracing a curious mindset, you turn ordinary moments into adventures. Whether you're taking a new route during your morning walk or checking out a local event, these little changes bring that travel excitement back home. It's like giving your regular life a sprinkle of wanderlust.

Also, travelling solo teaches you communication, resilience, and cultural awareness. These are tools that enrich both your professional and personal relationships. It's about capturing the essence of those travel vibes—like spontaneity and openness—and letting them reshape your everyday experiences. So, keep that travel spirit alive. Let it guide you toward new discoveries and connections right in your backyard.

In the final chapter, we'll keep talking about how travel can improve your daily life at home and encourage you to never stop learning. ∎

Iconic Landmarks

CHAPTER 15

Long-term benefits of solo travel

Travelling on your own unlocks a world of hidden treasures and experiences. Whether it's navigating bustling streets or finding solace in nature, each new journey leaves footprints within you and shapes you profoundly. If you're introverted or socially anxious, this concept may seem challenging initially. However, that's the beauty of travelling alone: It offers you the chance to grow at your own pace without the pressure of keeping up with someone else's expectations.

In the next few sections, we'll explore how travelling on your own is an opportunity for personal development. You'll find out how such experiences help you grow and become more flexible. Next, you'll discover how to build a toolkit of resources to use in your future travels. Finally, you'll learn how to keep learning and improving, thus always developing new skills.

Continue growing through new travels

Travelling alone allows you to understand and leverage the transformational effects of solo exploration. So, let's explore how solo travel builds your confidence, adaptability, and valuable life skills.

Firstly, being able to adapt to new environments is a crucial part of solo travel. When you navigate different cultures, you learn to build resilience and adaptability, qualities vital for facing future challenges. The experience of being in foreign lands with unfamiliar languages, customs, and societal norms compels you to become a keen observer and quick learner thinking on the spot. This immersion promotes resourcefulness as you assess situations and make informed decisions. Every country presents unique cultural settings, encouraging you to absorb and integrate diverse ways of life into your understanding to a level you feel comfortable with. Over time, these experiences cultivate comfort with change and boost your confidence in dealing with uncertainties.

Furthermore, your problem-solving improve significantly. As you explore new places, you're bound to face unexpected hurdles which require fast decision-making and troubleshooting. Therefore, each challenge you face enhances your ability to think on your feet. Such experiences instil a mindset of self-reliance, empowering you to trust your own instincts and judgement. By relying on yourself to resolve issues, you develop a greater sense of agency in your daily life, proving that you can handle whatever comes your way.

Another major benefit is the enhancement of communication skills. Travelling on your own means engaging with a variety of individuals from different backgrounds, whether it's fellow travellers at a hostel, locals in a bustling marketplace or people in professional and authoritative positions. Each new encounter sharpens your interpersonal skills, making you better at initiating conversations, listening actively, and empathising with others' perspectives, beliefs and situation. These interactions often lead to building meaningful connections and friendships, opening doors to new opportunities both personally and professionally. The ability to effectively communicate across cultural and linguistic barriers enriches your travel experience and deepens your understanding of global diversity, thus making it easier to embark on new adventures. As your confidence grows, you will feel your comfort zone gradually expanding as well as being able to see the bigger picture.

In addition, you develop a new independence. When you travel alone, you have the freedom to tailor your itinerary, make spontaneous decisions, and follow your passions without having to accommodate others' preferences. This autonomy challenges you to step out of your comfort zone and encourages you to take risks you wouldn't normally take and set out on new endeavours. The more experiences you have, the more independent you become and the more you feel motivated to go on new adventures.

© Gordon Chesterman

...reflecting on your values...

Unlike group travel, where decisions are often shared, solo travel grants you full control over your experiences. This empowers you to embrace who you are and know yourself deeply. The more you travel, the more you'll find yourself reflecting on your values, goals, and aspirations away from the noise of normal everyday life. Such reflection enhances self-awareness and clarity about your path, thus encouraging personal growth and a stronger sense of identity. After a few travels, you will have developed this new identity made of confidence, independence, and flexibility. In other words, you explore new dimensions of yourself. In fact, travel pushes you to try activities you might not have considered in familiar settings. Every new task helps you redefine your boundaries and see the potential within yourself you never knew existed or knew were there, but we too nervous to bring them to the surface.

Becoming more flexible

As you'll learn during your trips, it's the unplanned moments that often turn into your most cherished and influencial memories. Solo travel teaches us to welcome the unexpected—not as disruptions to our itinerary but as invitations to new adventures. You might find a cosy local café while wandering lost in a foreign town or stumble upon an unknown festival. Each surprise carries the potential for excitement and learning, nudging you to remain open and adaptable.

CHAPTER 15

© Gordon Chesterman

Each new destination brings its unique set of circumstances and social cues, which can initially be very daunting. Navigating these differences emphasises not just adaptability but also empathy. When travelling alone, there's no one else to rely on for navigating misunderstandings or cultural faux pas—you learn by doing. This firsthand experience in adjusting to different cultures helps you develop a more inclusive mindset.

At the same time, mistakes are bound to happen when you are exploring unfamiliar places alone, especially if you've never been there before. Perhaps you missed a train because you misunderstood the schedule or ordered something unexpected off a menu due to language barriers. While mistakes might be frustrating at first, they are valuable teachers. Solo travel can provide ample space for introspection, allowing you to assess what didn't go to plan and how you could do better next time. Like anything you learn during life, this trial-and-error approach offers significant growth and guides your future journey. Gradually, you begin to embrace the idea that mistakes aren't failures but stepping stones toward personal development and self-confidence. No holiday ever goes the way you imagined. Something always happens to scupper the best laid plans. All you can do is accept what's happened, solve the problem and not go running to the hills screaming with your hair on fire. As you keep travelling, perceiving mistakes as opportunities becomes natural, and you accept every obstacle you encounter along the way.

Setting out on a solo holiday also means becoming an expert at creating backup plans. When you go on your travel, you may rarely know what exactly comes next. In such instances, having a plan B or even a C and D, becomes truly indispensable. This involves researching alternative routes, accommodations, or activities ahead of time. By wisely preparing for unpredictability, you reduce any anxiety and gain valuable self-confidence, knowing you are equipped to handle whatever new comes your way. The natural ability to formulate these backup strategies not only ensures a better travel experience but also translates into a vital life skill. It empowers you to navigate life's changing moments with a calm and collected mindset, thus reducing inner most fears and concerns in the long term.

Last but not least, having to tackle challenges on your own empowers you in ways that ripple through other areas of your life. When there's no one else to lean on, you learn to trust your instincts and make reasoned decisions easily and swiftly. This quality leads to increased self-reliance and teaches you to manage logistics and interactions without external validation. The independence gained from solo travel encourages you to take calculated risks and explore new opportunities. When you go on your own adventure for the first time, you might feel scared and insecure. You may doubt your decisions and wonder what's best in certain situations. As you keep travelling, you learn to listen to your gut feeling and trust it.

Building a toolkit of resources

Travel resources are essential for any trip, whether you're navigating through busy cities or remote areas. Apps such as Google Maps offer precise navigation, helping you find your way in unfamiliar environments, while TripIt or Kayak streamline your travel itinerary, keeping all trip details in one place. These digital helpers simplify planning processes, reducing the anxiety which is often associated with travel logistics. Moreover, they thrive on community networks, where fellow solo travellers share tips, reviews, and experiences. Websites such as hostels' networking sites promote connections, creating opportunities to join local events or find travel companions.

On the other hand, personal development aids complement travel experiences by fostering growth beyond the physical journey. Books touching on travel and self-improvement provide insights into personal strengths and weaknesses. Podcasts also introduce strategies and ideas that can enhance your outlook on life, building resilience and creativity. Finally, workshops and seminars, further add to the learning curve, offering structured environments for self-improvement whether they're in person or online. These resources serve as guides, enhancing your mental toolkit for both travel experiences and everyday challenges.

Managing anxiety, a common issue faced when travelling on your own or returning to familiar surroundings, is important. Coping strategies tailored for travel stress can have profound effects when back home. As you already learned, techniques such as deep breathing or mindfulness exercises will help emotional regulation, promoting calmness and clarity in chaotic situations. If you practise these methods regularly, you ensure they become second nature and offer solace during moments of unpredictability. Exercise, too, plays a role; even short walks or stretching routines significantly reduce stress levels, balancing emotional well-being. Finally, reflective practises, especially journalling, deepen the impact of solo travel. Keeping a travel journal allows you to record daily adventures, thoughts, and emotions so you can revisit them whenever you want.

If you started practising these strategies before travelling on your own, keep doing them whilst on the road. Once you come back home, let them become second nature by integrating them into your routine and transforming them into habits. This way, you build a toolkit of resources that will come in handy in all sorts of solo travel experiences.

© Gordon Chesterman

Continuous learning and self-improvement

As you venture into the unknown, each trip becomes a lesson in self-improvement. You'll find yourself adapting quickly and becoming more resourceful as you face various challenges alone. In turn, this self-reliance empowers you in other areas of life, too, making you more confident and open to continuous learning. Travelling through different cultures exposes you to new ways of thinking and encourages you to challenge your assumptions and broaden your horizons.

When you engage with diverse perspectives, the world becomes your classroom. Conversations with locals and fellow travellers are invaluable because they offer insights into their lives, beliefs, and experiences that you may not have encountered before. These interactions deepen your understanding of global issues and cultural nuances. At the same time, they help you see the world from varied viewpoints and enrich your own worldview. Finding common ground with people from different backgrounds builds empathy and opens up a sense of shared humanity.

The experiences you gain abroad don't just stay there; they shape who you come back home as. Perhaps you've discovered a passion for photography while exploring new landscapes or picked up culinary skills by taking a cooking class.

CHAPTER 15

Sharing these experiences through storytelling, projects, or social media may inspire others and keep your memories alive. If you apply the lessons learned during your travels, you might discover fulfilling hobbies and maybe even work opportunities, as I did in Tenerife with my photography and videography. I found work with a film company - FilmCanaryIslands - shooting BTS videos and stills photos - great fun! This then lead to working with Tornasol Films in Spain as 'Foto Fijas' (stills photographer), again, really enjoyable work. You never know where doors will lead.

Continue your personal growth, with feedback and reflection. Constructive criticism from trusted people and self-assessment will highlight areas for improvement and push you to evolve further. At the same time, reflecting on your experiences helps solidify them, allowing you to understand your strengths and identify weaknesses.

The beauty of solo travel lies in its transformative potential. From hesitant traveller to confident explorer, each journey feeds your development. The thrill of venturing into the unknown nurtures a mindset that embraces change and encourages fearlessness.

Travelling on your own is truly a transformative experience that redefines your whole self and opens up a world of possibilities.

In this chapter, you've explored how venturing alone encourages personal growth by pushing you out of your comfort zone. You've seen how travel enhances your adaptability and communication skills, making you more open to new ideas and perspectives. Each journey taken alone evolves your travel story and leaves a lasting impact on your everyday life.

As you reflect on what you experience and learn, take time to think about how venturing out on your own could be your pathway to feeling more empowered and discovering yourself on a deeper level. It's about accepting the unknown with curiosity and learning to trust yourself in any situation. The skills and perspectives gained on these adventures don't just stay overseas—they become an integral part of who you are, influencing how you approach life's challenges back home and in new travels. Each step outside your comfort zone brings you closer to understanding and leveraging the incredible effects of travelling alone. ■

CONCLUSION

Taking everything onboard

As you reach the end of this book, take a moment to pause and reflect on the journey you've embarked upon—not just within these pages but in your own life. Solo travel is transformative, and it holds a special power for those of us who have felt contained by our shyness or anxiety. You've been brave enough to consider stepping outside your comfort zone, and you should be proud of it!

Picture yourself returning home after your first solo adventure. As you sit quietly back on your sofa, perhaps with a cup of tea in hand, think back to those moments when you navigated a foreign city by yourself. Remember the mix of apprehension and excitement as you walked through unfamiliar streets. Maybe there was that initial fear of getting lost or making a mistake. But you persevered, didn't you? Now, as you recall that experience, you'll likely realise how it reshaped your confidence. You faced challenges head-on, and in doing so, discovered facets of your personality that may have previously been overshadowed by nervousness and doubt.

Solo travel isn't about reaching a destination; it's about embracing the journey itself and acknowledging your newfound freedom. There is something liberating about deciding your itinerary, changing plans at a whim if you feel like it, and immersing yourself wholly in each unique moment. Imagine standing atop a majestic mountain, feeling the crisp air fill your lungs, and knowing that you're there because you yourself chose to set out on this journey on your own. That sense of autonomy is powerful and influences how you approach life beyond travel. Whether it's starting a new project, meeting new people, or just taking a different route to work every now and then—you are exercising the same independence which solo travel fosters.

As you build upon these learning experiences, remember to carry the skills and courage you've nurtured into your daily life. Consider the little victories along your travels and let them inspire change at home. Perhaps when faced with mundane choices, such as selecting your morning coffee, you'll find yourself inspired by your adventures. Instead of sticking to a routine, why not venture into the uncharted, just as you did abroad? On a weekend, instead of having your morning coffee on the sofa as you normally do, break the routine and go into town to that busy cafe again and have it there. You might surprise yourself with what you'll discover, a newly awakened explorer's spirit ready to extend further boundaries or, even a future travel partner.

As I've mentioned, your journey doesn't end once you are back home in familiar surroundings. Rather, it's just the beginning of continued travels and exploration.

Motivation thrives on movement, and there's an entire world waiting out there. While the thought of stepping out again might seem daunting, remind yourself of the little victories and exhilaration from last adventure. The world is full of surprises, and just like those initial steps brought you unexpected happiness, so will your future travels.

Now, let's address the heart of the next chapter in your life: *What's stopping you from planning your next trip?* A world teeming with stories, cultures, and landscapes is out there waiting. With every new destination there are more opportunities to learn and grow. The unknown isn't something to fear but rather an invitation to expand your horizon and create your narrative.

Embrace your individuality. Your story is uniquely yours to tell. Just as many solo travellers before you have shaped their journeys, let nothing hold you back. The road ahead is vast, with infinite possibilities. One step at a time—that's all it takes to begin your next adventure.

I've watched many YouTube videos of people who travel the world on their own. If they've been doing it for a few years, it's interesting to watch their first video compared to their latest upload especially female bloggers. You'll see a difference in their personality as they've gained experience and confidence. This also reflects in their video production technique. They've developed a filming style and maybe invested in better cameras and mics to present more watchable videos. It's all part of the learning curve which they have embraced. They had to start somewhere. Taking that first step is huge, but once you take it, the personal discovery begins in an exciting way.

In closing, remember, courage is not the absence of fear but the willingness to confront it and move ahead. Each journey begins with a single decision to take that first step.

So, build your self-confidence, practise the exercises, choose your destination, book that ticket, pack your bags, and discover what it means to live freely—on your terms. If you don't have a dream destination, consider Singapore. I'm not being paid to suggest this a your destination, I just feel it's an ideal place to go as a testing ground to get you up and running on your first adventure. For me, it was a very personal and emotional trip. While there, I recalled the time I spent with my family on the RAF Changi airbase when I was just a kid and visited the places we used to live. I really felt a strong connection with Singapore and could easily imagine myself whizzing back in time, reliving the moments when I used to run around in shorts—no shirt or shoes—as the planes flew overhead. Before going back to Singapore, those memories were a fuzzy collection in my mind. All of a sudden, they all came flooding back, crystal clear.

In my case, visiting Singapore was very much a "bucket list" trip, and I plan to go back there to see the things I missed the last time, at least, that's my excuse! But Singapore not only brought back memories; it created new ones that pushed me to write this book. I believe it's the perfect place to start as a solo traveller, and I definitely recommend it for many reasons. Yes, it can be expensive, but with careful research, planning, and budgeting, it's well within anyone's pocket. Keep checking booking websites because there are always special offers being advertised.

Singapore is easy to get to with its many direct flights from all over the world. Getting around using public transport is not only safe but very reliable, convenient, and cheap. Another major reason to choose it is personal safety. I had no trouble exploring with expensive camera gear around my neck, even in the middle of the night. I saw many women out late and on their own, walking, sightseeing, taking photos, jogging and exercising. So, it's definitely a great venue for female solo travellers.

Everything from arranging my trip to getting there and negotiating immigration was a breeze because it's all automated. All you need is your passport, face, and thumb! The local people are very friendly and will gladly help if you need it. In particular, I found the hotel receptionists a goldmine for local information.

In general, I highly recommend Singapore as a destination to practise any of the various tips and techniques I've suggested. I never felt any stress or anxiety at any time, even when I forgot to close my room safe. Planning my daily itinerary using the local transport network, apps, and the hotel staff, was very easy indeed. Although my feet were absolutely screaming from all the walking, I returned home very relaxed and mentally energised with a tremendous sense of achievement, a lot more memories, a few videos and thousands of photos to edit! With all that said, new adventures are there for the taking. ∎

Now, the big question.

Will you push yourself forward, or will the comfort and safety of your sofa win once again?

REFERENCES

Sergii Pavlovskyi - AdobeStock

- Alton, L. (2017, May 19). 5 scientifically proven health benefits of travelling abroad. NBC News. www.nbcnews.com/better/wellness/5-scientifically-proven-health-benefits-traveling-abroad-n759631
- Aman, J. (2022, August 17). Travel bullet journal ideas and inspo. Page Flutter. pageflutter.com/travel-bullet-journal-ideas
- American Red Cross. (n.d.). Make a plan. Redcross.org. www.redcross.org/get-help/how-to-prepare-for-emergencies/make-a-plan.html
- Arghandewal, A. & Thomas, S. (2024, July 3). 8 best travel budget apps for your next vacation. Bankrate. www.bankrate.com/credit-cards/travel/best-travel-budget-apps
- Art & creativity for mental health & wellbeing + mixed media self-portrait process. (2021, December 24). Nela Dunato Art & Design. neladunato.com/blog/art-creativity-mental-health-mixed-media-portrait-process
- The art of flexible travel why planning only your first destination can lead to richer experiences. (2024, September 29). Mighty Travels Premium. www.mightytravels.com/2024/09/the-art-of-flexible-travel-why-planning-only-your-first-destination-can-lead-to-richer-experiences
- Artful retreats. (n.d.). ArtfulRetreats. www.artfulretreats.com
- Baker, D. (2023, March 11). How to make friends with local people when traveling. Wendy Perrin. www.wendyperrin.com/how-to-make-friends-with-local-people-when-traveling
- Bell, L. (2024, August 20). Best hotel booking sites - and the cheapest. Which? www.which.co.uk/reviews/travel-agents/article/travel-agents/best-and-worst-hotel-booking-websites-aurVF5V9U33P
- Benefits of learning another language! (n.d.). LanguageBird. www.languagebird.com/benefits-of-learning-another-language
- Berg, B. (2024, April 17). The 15 best travel safety devices 2024, tested by a frequent solo traveler. Forbes. www.forbes.com/sites/forbes-personal-shopper/article/best-travel-safety-devices
- The best gear for travel. (2024, August 19). New York Times. www.nytimes.com/wirecutter/reviews/travel-guide
- Best travel websites. (n.d.). Worldtrips. www.worldtrips.com/resources/best-travel-websites
- Better Health Channel. (n.d.). Strong relationships, strong health. www.betterhealth.vic.gov.au/health/HealthyLiving/Strong-relationships-strong-health
- Bhowmik, S. (2023, April 24). How to stay healthy while traveling. MedicalNewsToday. www.medicalnewstoday.com/articles/how-to-stay-healthy-while-traveling
- Blasche, G., deBloom, J., Chang, A., & Pichlhoefer, O. (2021, February 8). Is a meditation retreat the better vacation? effect of retreats and vacations on fatigue, emotional well-being, and acting with awareness (S. Hoefer, Ed.). PLOS ONE. doi.org/10.1371/journal.pone.0246038
- Bowen, S., Elliott, S., & Brenton, J. (2014, August). The Joy of Cooking? Journals of the American Sociological Association. doi.org/10.1177/1536504214545755
- Brenneman, K. (2023, July 12). The healing power of travel: How exploring the world can benefit mental health. Painted Brain. paintedbrain.org/blog/lifestyle/the-healing-power-of-travel-how-exploring-the-world-can-benefit-mental-health
- Brenneman, K. (2024, March 18). How to practice cultural sensitivity during meaningful travel. GoAbroad.com. www.goabroad.com/articles/how-to-practice-cultural-sensitivity
- Carmin, C. (2024, October 23). 5 tips to ease pre-travel anxiety. The Ohio State University. wexnermedical.osu.edu/blog/pre-travel-anxiety
- Center for Disease Control and Prevention. (n.d.-a). Getting health care during travel. wwwnc.cdc.gov/travel/page/health-care-during-travel
- Center for Disease Control and Prevention. (n.d.-b). Obtaining health care abroad. wwwnc.cdc.gov/travel/yellowbook/2024/health-care-abroad/health-care-abroad
- Center for Disease Control and Prevention. (n.d.-c). Your survival guide to safe and healthy travel. wwwnc.cdc.gov/travel/page/survival-guide
- Cherry, K. (2024, March 26). Things to do by yourself. Verywell Mind. www.verywellmind.com/the-benefits-of-being-by-yourself-4769939
- Claire. (2023, August 9). 13 benefits of solo travel that will change your life. Tales of a Backpacker. talesofabackpacker.com/benefits-of-solo-travel/
- Connect in a crisis: Emergency communication guide. (n.d.). SafetyIQ. safetyiq.com/insight/connect-in-a-crisis-emergency-communication-guide
- Connor, B. (n.d.). Travelers' diarrhea. Center for Disease Control and Prevention. wwwnc.cdc.gov/travel/yellowbook/2024/preparing/travelers-diarrhea
- Copley, L. (2023, November 30). 30 best journaling prompts for improving mental health. PositivePsychology.com. positivepsychology.com/journaling-prompts
- Creativity affirmations. (2021, February 8). Bergreen Photography. www.bergreenphotography.com/creativity-affirmations
- Curtiss, J. E., Levine, D. S., Ander, I., & Baker, A. W. (2021, June 17). Cognitive-behavioral treatments for anxiety and stress-related disorders. Focus. doi.org/10.1176/appi.focus.20200045
- Deep journal prompts for personal growth & self-improvement. (2023, April 2). Sage & Bloom. sageandbloom.co/journal-prompts-for-personal-growth-self-improvement
- Delarato, L. (2017, November 21). Why travelling alone is the best impulse decision I ever made. NBC News. www.nbcnews.com/better/health/why-travelling-alone-best-impulse-decision-i-ever-made-ncna821526
- Dembling, S. (2017, March 11). The peculiar pleasures of traveling alone. Psychology Today. www.psychologytoday.com/intl/blog/the-introverts-corner/201703/the-peculiar-pleasures-of-traveling-alone
- Derek. (2013, May 23). Ordinary people & their inspiring travel stories. Wandering Earl. wanderingearl.com/ordinary-people-their-inspiring-travel-stories
- Detroy. (2024, September 23). Solo travel for ADHD. Medium. medium.com/@Detroy/solo-travel-for-adhd-91b01793cb81
- Developing self-reliance: how to be comfortable with being alone. (2024, August 16). ImPossible Psychological Services. www.impossiblepsychservices.com.sg/our-resources/articles/2024/08/16/developing-self-reliance-how-to-be-comfortable-with-being-alone
- Dulis, P. (2020, December 3). How to evoke emotion with landscape photography. Visual Wilderness. visualwilderness.com/composition-creativity/how-to-evoke-emotion-with-landscape-photography
- 8 practical tips to overcome the unexpected hurdles of solo travel. (2024). Mighty Travels Premium. www.mightytravels.com/2024/06/8-practical-tips-to-overcome-the-unexpected-hurdles-of-solo-travel
- The era of spontaneous travel: Why 2024 is the year of impromptu adventures. (2024, September 13). Lugos Travel. lugostravel.com/blog/the-era-of-spontaneous-travel-why-2024-is-the-year-of-impromptu-adventures/
- Essie. (2024, January 27). Budgeting for travel: How to explore more for less. Be Your Own Travel Guide. beyourowntravelguide.com/budgeting-for-travel-made-easy-how-to-explore-more-for-less
- Estis, R. (2020, September 10). 5 journaling prompts to build resilience. Ryan Estis. ryanestis.com/5-journaling-prompts-to-build-emotional-resilience
- Fagan, D. (n.d.). Journal prompts & ideas for emotional release. My TMS Journey. mytmsjourney.com/resources/journal-prompts-ideas-for-emotional-release
- Geller, E. (2024, August 12). 8 safety tips for solo female travel. NerdWallet. www.nerdwallet.com/article/travel/solo-female-travel-tips
- Gibbson, A. (2024, March 30). How solitude transforms us: The unseen power of embracing alone time. AndrewGGibson. andrewggibson.com/2024/03/30/embracing-solitude-for-mental-health
- A guide to travel photography - How to take better travel photos part 1. (n.d.). TravelPixelz. www.travelpixelz.com/blog/travel-photography-guide-pt1
- Habitat for Humanity. (n.d.). Disaster preparedness: Family communications plan. www.habitat.org/our-work/disaster-response/disaster-preparedness-homeowners/family-communications-plan

- Harvard Health. (2024, October 4). Benefits of mindfulness. HelpGuide.org. www.helpguide.org/mental-health/stress/benefits-of-mindfulness
- Helke, L. (2024, August). Mastering solo travel: tips for women facing anxiety. Lori Loves Adventure. lorilovesadventure.com/mastering-solo-travel-tips-women-anxiety
- Hofmann, S. G., & Gómez, A. F. (2017). Mindfulness-based interventions for anxiety and depression. Psychiatric Clinics of North America. doi.org/10.1016/j.psc.2017.08.008
- Hokanson, C. (2020, April 22). Sharing your travel story to inspire & empower others. Her Packing List. herpackinglist.com/sharing-your-story
- Hossain, K. I. (2024). Reviewing the role of culture in English language learning: Challenges and opportunities for educators. Social Sciences & Humanities Open. doi.org/10.1016/j.ssaho.2023.100781
- How a solo travel can improve your wellness and contribute to your personal growth. (2023, March 14). Fault. fault-magazine.com/2023/03/how-a-solo-travel-can-improve-your-wellness-and-contribute-to-your-personal-growth
- How anxiety leads to irrational fears and 5 ways to cope. (n.d.). Mind Health Group. www.mindhealthgroup.com/blog/how-anxiety-leads-to-irrational-fears-ways-to-cope
- How to keep your travel itinerary loose and have an incredible vacation. (n.d.). Wonder & Sundry. wonderandsundry.com/how-to-keep-your-travel-itinerary-loose-and-have-an-incredible-vacation
- How to set and achieve goals with journaling. (n.d.). ErinCondren. www.erincondren.com/inspiration-center-journaling-goals?srsltid=AfmBOop7UU-mS4mGEWNp9cvrS7_iMp_PyBZrTorqTo6ZOMEQ0BixOtX4
- How to travel on a budget: 17 ways to save money. (2024, April 22). Everki. www.everki.com/ch_en/everki-stories/travel-on-a-budget.html
- Importance of cultural awareness: Everything to know. (n.d.). Impactly. www.getimpactly.com/post/importance-of-cultural-awareness
- Improve travel with mindful seeing and the art of noticing. (n.d.). Travel Bug Tonic. www.travelbugtonic.com/blog/mindful-seeing
- Jesih, J. (2022, March 7). Solo female travel: independence, empowerment, personal growth and resilience. Jaki en Fuerte. jakionfuerte.com/solo-female-travel-independence-empowerment-personal-growth-and-resilience
- Jordan, N. (2023, May 16). Things you should know before first solo trip, from repeat traveler. Business Insider. www.businessinsider.com/solo-travel-things-to-know-before-first-trip
- Joseph. (2024, October 16). Empowering women travel: How exploring the world builds confidence. LaKat's Global. lakatsglobal.org/empowering-women-travel-how-exploring-the-world-builds-confidence
- Katie. (2020, May 5). How to use travel affirmations for your solo trip. Just Chasing Sunsets. www.justchasingsunsets.com/travel-affirmations
- Kimberli. (2024, August 21). 11 tips for making friends while traveling alone. Worldpackers. www.worldpackers.com/articles/tips-for-making-friends-while-traveling-alone
- Last, F. (2023, October 6). 11 undeniable benefits of solo travel. GoAbroad.com. www.goabroad.com/articles/benefits-of-solo-travel
- Mataković, H., & Cunjak Mataković, I. (2019). The impact of crime on security in tourism. Security and Defence Quarterly, 27(5), 1-20. doi.org/10.35467/sdq/115559
- McMennamy, A. (2024, June 13). Travel with confidence: How GPS trackers prevent lost luggage. Tracki. tracki.com/es/blogs/post/how-gps-trackers-prevent-lost-luggage?srsltid=AfmBOopq7kOSICBPfFtYAhfSXhDBYGT0P9tDrJshIzzTmpYvNQw-q3EI
- Mindful Staff. (n.d.). How to manage stress with mindfulness and meditation. Mindful. www.mindful.org/how-to-manage-stress-with-mindfulness-and-meditation
- Moe, K. (2021, June 4). 5 visualization techniques to help you reach your goals. Betterup. www.betterup.com/blog/visualization
- Mount Sinai (n.d.). Traveler's diarrhea diet. www.mountsinai.org/health-library/nutrition/traveler-s-diarrhea-diet
- Nantes, T. (n.d.). 35 best travel planning tools and apps. Travels with Talek. travelswithtalek.com/15-best-travel-planning-tools-and-apps
- Otegui-Carles, A., Araújo-Vila, N., & Fraiz-Brea, J. A. (2022, August 23). Solo travel research and its gender perspective: A critical bibliometric review. Tourism and Hospitality. doi.org/10.3390/tourhosp3030045
- Pendergast, D. (2023, July 26). Travel 101: Our favorite hacks, hints and how-tos. The New York Times. www.nytimes.com/explain/2023/travel-hacks-tips
- Projects Abroad. (2024, February 8). Solo female travel: Fall in love with traveling alone. www.projects-abroad.org/blog/solo-travel-for-women
- Purkayastha, R. (2023, April 23). The benefits of nature on mental health: tips for connecting with the outdoors. Medium. medium.com/@mail2rajashree/nature-the-ultimate-prescription-for-mental-wellness-1faa886eb8a1
- Russell, C. (2023, August 30). What are the psychological benefits of travelling alone? The Travel Psychologist. thetravelpsychologist.co.uk/benefits-of-travel/f/what-are-the-psychological-benefits-of-travelling-alone
- Russell, C. (2024, August 7). How can travel help with our personal growth? The Travel Psychologist. thetravelpsychologist.co.uk/benefits-of-travel/f/travel-personal-growth
- Schuman-Olivier, Z., Trombka, M., Lovas, D. A., Brewer, J. A., Vago, D. R., Gawande, R., Dunne, J. P., Lazar, S. W., Loucks, E. B., & Fulwiler, C. (2020). Mindfulness and behavior change. Harvard Review of Psychiatry. doi.org/10.1097/HRP.0000000000000277
- Shipanga, K., R. (2024, March 26). 9 strategies for making friends while traveling. GoAbroad.com. www.goabroad.com/articles/how-to-make-friends-while-traveling
- Sims, S. (2023, July 26). The friend trip: Fun without the friction. The New York Times. www.nytimes.com/2023/07/26/travel/plan-friend-trip.html
- Slow morning routine #1: Bullet journaling to focus and turbocharge your day. (2020, June 5). Nomad Numbers. www.nomadnumbers.com/how-5-minutes-of-bullet-journaling-can-help-you-focus-and-turbocharge-your-day
- Solo travel as a tool for career growth. (2024, October 7). Exploresololife. exploresololife.blog/solo-travel-as-a-tool-for-career-growth
- Solo travel holidays. (n.d.). Exodus. www.exodustravels.com/way-to-travel/solo-traveller-holidays
- Solo travel on a budget money-saving strategies for independent explorers. (n.d.). ConnectPls. connectpls.com/solo-travel-on-a-budget-money-saving-strategies-for-independent-explorers
- Somanathan, S. (2024, September 1). How to create the perfect itinerary for your trip. ClickUp. clickup.com/blog/how-to-make-an-itinerary
- Springfield Police (n.d.). Public transportation safety tips. www.springfieldmo.gov/307/Public-Transportation-Safety-Tips
- Susan. (n.d.). Travel essentials for women. Midlife Globetrotter. midlifeglobetrotter.com/travel-essentials-for-women
- Talajia, S. (2024, August 7). How to maintain a healthy lifestyle while traveling. Grabenord. grabenord.com/blogs/blog/how-to-maintain-a-healthy-lifestyle-while-traveling?srsltid=AfmBOopUgTIA8DaMyZI3aqEqF5CgGzdjOA4MIdWxk8blIpnD3Z-VeiBE
- Tan, A. (2023, December 17). How to choose a travel destination. WikiHow. www.wikihow.com/Choose-a-Travel-Destination
- Teng, Y.-M., Wu, K.-S., & Lee, Y.-C. (2023, January 4). Do personal values and motivation affect women's solo travel intentions in Taiwan? Humanities and Social Sciences Communications. doi.org/10.1057/s41599-022-01499-5
- The 10-step guide to setting & achieving your travel goals. (2021, July 27). Conquest Maps. www.conquestmaps.com/blogs/the-compass/how-to-clarify-achieve-your-travel-goals?srsltid=AfmBOorvH4C9hb4_Sm52ozsO5v8p6XNu2W96M-s3yCTSmGaK5dpeEnnT
- Toy, R. (2024, October 17). 7 ways to make travel less stressful. National Geographic. www.nationalgeographic.com/travel/article/travel-anxiety-expert-tips
- Trappett, L. (2023, September 11). 10 tips to encourage community engagement in diverse communities. Social Pinpoint. www.socialpinpoint.com/10-tips-to-encourage-community-engagement-in-diverse-communities
- Traveling culture: A best deep dive into the global phenomenon in 2024. (2024, September 5). Travel Trips. traveltrips.io/traveling-culture
- 2024 solo female travel trends & statistics. (2024). Solo Female Travelers. www.solofemaletravelers.club/solo-female-travel-stats
- Ultimate guide to safe and healthy family travel. (n.d.). WorldTrips. www.worldtrips.com/resources/safe-family-travel
- Understanding situational awareness: The key to personal and professional safety. (2024, September 27). Active Crisis. activecrisis.com/understanding-situational-awareness
- University of Notre Dame. (n.d.). Safety & security. global.nd.edu/travel-safety/travel-health-safety-and-security/safety/safety-and-security
- The University of Texas at Austin. (2024, June 26). Top tips for stress-free air travel. sites.utexas.edu/discovery/2024/06/26/top-tips-for-stress-free-air-travel
- Wiki Voyage. (n.d.). Common scams. en.wikivoyage.org/wiki/Common_scams
- Wilde, D. (2024, May 21). The mental health benefits of green spaces: Nature's therapy. Espyr. www.espyr.com/blog/the-mental-health-benefits-of-green-spaces-natures-therapy
- Women's travel safety. (n.d.). Travel Guard. www.travelguard.com/travel-resources/travel-safety/womens-travel-safety
- WomensMedia. (2021, January 15). The benefits of resting and how to unplug in a busy world. Forbes. www.forbes.com/sites/womensmedia/2021/01/15/the-benefits-of-resting-and-how-to-unplug-in-a-busy-world
- Your trusted choice for solo travel. (n.d.). G Adventures. www.gadventures.com/solo-travel

Useful Notes

Names & Addresses

Published 2025 - PinkbeeBooks
ISBN: 978-1-7397688-8-1
© Copyright 2025 - All rights reserved.

Author: Gordon Chesterman
Cover illustration, Design & Layout: Gordon Chesterman

The content contained within this book may not be reproduced, duplicated or transmitted without direct written permission from the author or the publisher.
Under no circumstances will any blame or legal responsibility be held against the publisher, or author, for any damages, reparation, or monetary loss due to the information contained within this book, either directly or indirectly.

Legal Notice:
This book is copyright protected. It is only for personal use. You cannot amend, distribute, sell, use, quote or paraphrase any part, or the content within this book, without the consent of the author or publisher.

Disclaimer Notice:
Please note the information contained within this document is for educational and entertainment purposes only. All effort has been executed to present accurate, up to date, reliable, complete information. No warranties of any kind are declared or implied. Readers acknowledge that the author is not engaged in the rendering of legal, financial, medical or professional advice. The content within this book has been derived from various sources. Please consult a licensed professional before attempting any techniques outlined in this book.
By reading this document, the reader agrees that under no circumstances is the author responsible for any losses, direct or indirect, that are incurred as a result of the use of the information contained within this document, including, but not limited to, errors, omissions, or inaccuracies.

www.pinkbeebooks.com

www.ingramcontent.com/pod-product-compliance
Lightning Source LLC
Chambersburg PA
CBHW061119070526
44583CB00028B/3343